AFFIRMATION STATION

Helpful Hints for the Human Heart

*For Ronnie & Max
I hope this book is
a blessing to you both!*

Love, Ed Lannin

ED LANNIN

ISBN 978-1-64492-154-8 (paperback)
ISBN 978-1-64492-921-6 (hardcover)
ISBN 978-1-64492-155-5 (digital)

Copyright © 2019 by Ed Lannin

All rights reserved. No part of this publication may be reproduced, distributed, or transmitted in any form or by any means, including photocopying, recording, or other electronic or mechanical methods without the prior written permission of the publisher. For permission requests, solicit the publisher via the address below.

Christian Faith Publishing, Inc.
832 Park Avenue
Meadville, PA 16335
www.christianfaithpublishing.com

Printed in the United States of America

INTRODUCTION

When we are blessed to receive the Word of God, we are warned of a couple pitfalls that can await us. According to Matthew 13, one thing that may occur is that "the wicked One comes and snatches away what was sown in our heart." Another problem we can face is doubt, if our lives are not grounded in the word of life. We can be tricked into going down a dangerous path by listening to "Did God really say that?" It is with the hope of eliminating these obstacles to the fruitful life of living by God's Word that I have put together this book of daily devotional verse trains.

My approach was to select a hundred-plus life situations and combine three or more Bible verses about each area. By looking at each subject exclusively from several vantage points, we should get a clearer in-depth view. As you read these verses individually and as a group, my hope is that you will receive strength from their unity, like a three-strand cord, which is not quickly broken (Ecclesiastes 4:12), while also being built up and encouraged.

Whether you are beginning your spiritual journey of growing in grace or are seeking to return to your first love, may this comforting and correcting collection of verses, by letting Scripture confirm Scripture, help you let the "Word of Christ dwell in you richly" (Colossians 3:16), so "that you may grow thereby" (1 Peter 2:1–2). Importantly in this regard is that we ask for and trust the Holy Spirit, who is given to those who believe (1 Corinthians 2:12) to guide us into all truth, knowing He will seek to glorify Jesus, "the author and finisher of our faith" (Hebrews 12:2). We do well to request wisdom from God, since He assures us He does and will answer our prayer for it (James 1:5) and lets us also ask for Jesus to "open our understanding to comprehend the Scriptures" (Luke 24:45).

I pray this book, by planting the Word generously, will help you know more of what the Lord thinks and feels, so you can walk in agreement with Him, for how "can two walk together, unless they are agreed?" (Amos 3:3). May we all be "doers of the word and not hearers only" (James 1:21–22), "being no longer conformed to the pattern of this world" (Romans 12:2) but be "partakers in God's promises" (1 Peter 1:4), "having been born again, not of corruptible seed but incorruptible, through the word of God which lives and abides forever" (1 Peter 1:23).

CONTENTS

1. Casting Cares And Cultivating Contentment 9
2. Treasures from Trust 10
3. Worry Worsens 11
4. Forever Firm Foundation 12
5. Doing What He Says Proves We Believe What He Says 13
6. Learning to Listen 14
7. Who We Are 15
8. Whole Heart Finds Holy Lord 16
9. Making too Much of Money 17
10. The Lost Virtue of Gentleness 18
11. Babies Know Best 19
12. Armed with the Lord's Strength 20
13. Watching Our Words 21
14. Having Humility Helps 23
15. The Lord Hears 24
16. Life in His Loving Look 25
17. Day by Day Is God's Way 27
18. Avoiding Anxiety 28
19. Fruitful with Our Lips 29
20. Assessable Affirmation 30
21. Corrected, Not Condemned 32
22. Trading Trauma for Double Honor 33
23. Fully Forgiven Forever 34
24. God's Gracious Guidance 35
25. Preserved to Be Presented Faultless 37
26. Choosing Wisdom Over Wealth 38
27. Poor Plan to Trust in Man 39
28. The Lazy Lose 40

29.	From Tears to Triumph	41
30.	Minding Our Own Matters	42
31.	Our Precious Priest	43
32.	Providing the Poor with Plenty	44
33.	Wonderful if We'd Walk in His Ways	45
34.	Letting His Peace Rule	47
35.	Not Law or Works, but Grace through Faith	48
36.	Our Saving Shield	50
37.	Courageous, for You Are with Us	51
38.	Walking Humbly with Your God	52
39.	A Heavenly Hug	53
40.	Faith in Christ Brings and Keeps Life	54
41.	The Word Does Good	55
42.	Loving Brings Assurance	56
43.	Our Gracious, Giving God	58
44.	Blessed be God Forever	59
45.	Assured, Strengthened, Helped, And Upheld	60
46.	Sealed by the Spirit to Walk in the Spirit	62
47.	Make Me Faithful-Hearted Me	64
48.	The Lord, Strong and Mighty	65
49.	Settling Our Souls	66
50.	Mighty Meaningful to be Merciful!	67
51.	Finding Freedom	68
52.	Waiting in Your Wings	70
53.	Our Own Wickedness Will Correct Us	71
54.	Trusting and Triumphing through Tribulation	72
55.	Guarding Goodness	74
56.	The Best Is Yet to Come	75
57.	If You Would Be Royalty, Treat People Royally	77
58.	Not Facing Temptation Alone	78
59.	Letting the Word Do Its Work	79
60.	How Chic to Be Meek	80
61.	Saved from Shame	81
62.	His Upholding Right Hand	83
63.	Heaven, Our Home	85
64.	A Future and a Hope	87

65. Planted In Perfect Peace	88
66. Encouraged to Add and Pursue	90
67. It Works to Wait	92
68. Making Your Heart His	94
69. Established Eternally	95
70. Afflicted to Be Liberated	97
71. A Little Is a Lot with the Lord	99
72. To Be Acceptable in Your Sight	100
73. Watching Out for Wolves	101
74. The Lord, Our Champion	102
75. Greatly Grateful for Your Wonderous Works	103
76. Love, Rich and Everlasting	104
77. Nothing Hidden that Won't Be Revealed	105
78. Not Being Bent on a Bad Bargain	107
79. Forever, Even Forever And Ever	108
80. Clean Courage	109
81. Praise and Partake of His Perfect Power	110
82. Preserved and Guarded in Christ	111
83. Shielding and Sheltering Savior	112
84. The Lord Our Righteousness	113
85. Partaking In His Promises	114
86. Leaning on the Lord Lights the Way	116
87. Divinely Drawn	117
88. Accepting Alterations	118
89. Problematic but Protected People	119
90. Putting Our Love to Work	121
91. Lord God, Rock of Life	122
92. Friend Or Foe, Forewarned Is Forearmed	124
93. Oh, That God's People Would Praise Him!	126
94. Hungering for the Right Things	128
95. Including Thanksgiving In and For Everything	130
96. Being Return Ready	132
97. Loved by the Father and the Son. Amen!	134
98. No Shame in Serving	136
99. Prayer, More Than A Plus	138
100. Abundant Redemption	140

101. Salvation from the Savior 142
102. Being Made New 143
103. Sing of His Great Goodness 144
104. From Trouble to Trust 145
105. Exceeding Inexpressible Joy 146
106. Mind Yourself 148
107. Forever and Forward Focused 150
108. Brought Near, Cleansed, Forgiven, and God's Own 152
109. Betrothed Beloved Bride 154
110. Together for Good 156
111. Safe, Restored, and Rested 157
112. Tell Them what Great Things the Lord has Done 158

CASTING CARES AND CULTIVATING CONTENTMENT

Cast all your care upon Him, for He cares for you (*1 Peter 5:7*). The LORD is my shepherd; I shall not want. He makes me to lie down in green pastures; He leads me beside the still waters. He restores my soul (*Psalm 23:1–3*). Surely I have calmed and quieted my soul, like a weaned child with his mother; like a weaned child is my soul within me (*Psalm 131:2*). He who is greedy for gain troubles his own house (*Proverbs 15:27*). And having food and clothing, with these we shall be content (*1 Timothy 6:8*). Let your conduct be without covetousness; be content with such things as you have. For He Himself has said, "I will never leave you nor forsake you" so we may boldly say: "The LORD is my helper: I will not fear. What can man do to me?" (*Hebrews 13:5–6*). Godliness with contentment is great gain (*1 Timothy 6:6*). For I have learned in whatever state I am, to be content (*Philippians 4:1*). Not that we are sufficient of ourselves to think of anything as being from ourselves, but our sufficiency is from God (*2 Corinthians 3:5*). Be anxious for nothing, but in everything by prayer and supplication, with thanksgiving, let your requests be made known to God; and the peace of God, which surpasses all understanding, will guard your hearts and minds through Christ Jesus (*Philippians 4:6-7*). The LORD is your keeper (*Psalm 121:5*).

TREASURES FROM TRUST

"Blessed is the man who trusts in the LORD, and whose hope is the LORD (*Jeremiah 17:7*). He who trusts in the LORD, mercy shall surround him (*Psalm 32:10*). He heeded their prayer, because they put their trusted in Him (*1 Chronicles 5:20*). Oh, taste and see that the LORD is good; blessed is the man who trusts in Him! (*Psalm 34:8*). He [the LORD] knows those who trust in Him (*Nahum 1:7*). None of those who trust in Him shall be condemned (*Psalm 34:22*). Blessed is the man who makes the LORD his trust (*Psalm 40:4*). Those who trust in the LORD are like Mount Zion, which cannot be moved, but abides forever (*Psalm 125:1*). Whoever trusts in the LORD, happy is he (*Proverbs 16:20*). He who trusts in the LORD will be prospered (*Proverbs 28:25*). Whoever trusts in the LORD will be safe (*Proverbs* 29:25). He is a shield to all who trust in Him (*Psalm 18:30*). The LORD is my strength and shield; my heart trusted in Him, and I am helped (*Psalm 28:7*). Let all those rejoice who put their trust in You; let them ever shout for joy, because You defend them (*Psalm 5:11*). "Your life shall be a prize to you, because you have put your trust in Me, says the LORD" (*Jeremiah 39:18*). "Let not your heart be troubled; you believe in God, believe also in Me [Jesus]. In My Father's house are many mansions; if it were not so, I would have told you. I go to prepare a place for you. And if I go and prepare a place for you, I will come again and receive you to Myself; that where I am, there you may be also" (1 Peter 14:1–3).

WORRY WORSENS

Do not fret because of evildoers... Trust in the Lord, and do good... Commit your way to the LORD, trust also in Him... Rest in the LORD, and wait patiently for Him; do not fret because of him who prospers in his way, because of the man who brings wicked schemes to pass. Cease from anger, and forsake wrath; do not fret—it only causes harm. For evildoers shall be cut off; but those who wait upon the LORD, they shall inherit the earth... Depart from evil, and do good; and dwell forevermore. For the LORD loves justice, and does not forsake His saints *(Psalm 37:1–28)*. But the very hairs of your head are all numbered *(Matthew 10:30)*. Therefore I say to you, do not worry about your life, what you will eat or what you will drink, nor about your body, what you will put on. Is not life more than food and the body more than clothing? Look at the birds of the air, for they neither sow nor reap nor gather into barns; yet your heavenly Father feeds them. Are you not of more value than they? Which of you by worrying can add one cubit to his stature? So why do you worry about clothing? Consider the lilies of the field, how they grow: they neither toil nor spin; and yet I say to you that even Solomon in all his glory was not arrayed like one of these... Your heavenly Father knows that you need all these things. But seek first the kingdom of God, and His righteousness, and all these things shall be added to you. Therefore do not worry about tomorrow, for tomorrow will worry about its own things. Sufficient for the day is its own trouble *(Matthew 6:25–34)* Nor have an anxious mind *(Luke 12:29)*. "So I say to you, ask and it will be given to you; seek, and you will find; knock, and it will be opened to you. For everyone who asks receives, and he who seeks finds, and to him who knocks it will be opened *(Luke 11:9-10)."*

FOREVER FIRM FOUNDATION

Therefore thus says the Lord God: "Behold, I lay in Zion a stone for a foundation, a tried stone, a precious cornerstone, a sure foundation; whoever believes will not act hastily (*Isaiah 28:16*). You are no longer strangers,…but members of the household of God, having been built on the foundation of the apostles and prophets, Jesus Christ Himself being the chief cornerstone (*Ephesians 2:19–20*). Nevertheless the solid foundation of God stands, having this seal: "The Lord knows those who are His" and "Let everyone who names the name of Christ depart from iniquity" (*2 Timothy 2:19*). The righteous has an everlasting foundation (*Proverbs 10:25*). Whoever comes to me, and hears my sayings and does them, I will show you whom he is like: He is like a man building a house, who dug deep and laid the foundation on the rock, and when the flood arose, the stream beat vehemently against that house, and could not shake it, for it was founded on the rock (*Luke 6:46–48*). You are God's building. According to the grace of God which was given to me (the Apostle Paul), as a wise master builder I have laid the foundation, and another builds on it. But let each one take heed how he builds on it. For no other foundation can anyone lay than that, which is laid, which is Jesus Christ (*1 Corinthians 3:9–11*).

DOING WHAT HE SAYS PROVES WE BELIEVE WHAT HE SAYS

"But why do you call Me 'Lord, Lord,' and do not the things which I say?" (*Luke 6:46*). But be doers of the word, and not hears only, deceiving yourselves (*James 1:22*). Let no one deceive you. He who practices righteousness is righteous, just as He is righteous (*1 John 3:7*). In this the children of God and the children of the devil are manifest: Whoever does not practice righteousness is not of God, nor is he who does not love his brother (*1 John 3:10*). And whoever orders his conduct aright I will show the salvation of God (*Psalm 50:23*). We know that we have passed from death to life, because we love the brethren. He who does not love his brother abides in death (*1 John 3:14*). By this we know we that we know him, if we keep His commandments [to love God and one another] He who says, "I know Him," and does not keep his commandments is a liar, and the truth is not in him. But he who keeps his word, truly the love of God is perfected in Him. By this we know that we are in Him (*1 John 2:3–4*). My little children, let us not love in word or in tongue, but in deed and truth. And by this we know that we are of the truth, and shall assure our hearts before Him (*1 John 3:18–19*). And may the Lord make you increase and abound in love to one another and to all, just as we do to you, so He may establish your hearts blameless in holiness before our God and Father at the coming of our Lord Jesus Christ with all His saints (*1 Thessalonians 3:12-13*).

LEARNING TO LISTEN

Hear, O My people. And I will admonish you! (*Psalm 81:8*). Oh, that My people would listen to Me, that Israel would walk in My ways (*Psalm 81:13*). Incline your ear and hear the words of the wise, apply your heart to my knowledge; for it is a pleasant thing if you keep them within you, let them be fixed upon your lips, so that your trust may be in the LORD (*Proverbs 22:17–19*). Now therefore, listen to me, my children, for blessed are those who keep my ways. Hear instruction and be wise (*Proverbs 8:32–33*). A wise man will hear and increase learning (*Proverbs 1:5*). But whoever listens to me [wisdom] will dwell safely, and will be secure without fear of evil (*Proverbs 1:33*). So then faith comes by hearing, and hearing by the word of God (*Romans 10:17*). For by faith you stand (*2 Corinthians 1:24*). So then, my beloved brethren, let every man be swift to hear, slow to speak, slow to wrath; for the wrath of man does not produce the righteousness of God (*James 1:19–20*). Listen carefully to Me, and eat what is good, and let your soul delight itself in abundance. Incline your ear, and come to Me. Hear and your soul shall live (*Isaiah 55:2–3*). Listen to counsel and receive instruction, that you may be wise in your latter days (*Proverbs 19:20*). My [Jesus] sheep hear My voice, and I know them, and they follow Me. And I give them eternal life, and they shall never perish; neither shall anyone snatch them out of My hand (*John 10:27–28*).

WHO WE ARE

You are a chosen generation, a royal priesthood, a holy nation, His own special people, that you may proclaim the praises of Him who called you out of darkness into His marvelous light; who once were not a people but are now the people of God, who had not obtained mercy but now have obtained mercy (*1 Peter 2:9–10*). In Him we have redemption through His blood, the forgiveness of sins, according to the riches of His grace (*Ephesians 1:7*). That having been justified by His grace we should become heirs according to the hope of eternal life (*Titus 3:7*). Whoever believes that Jesus is the Christ is born of God (*1 John 5:1*). For you are all sons of God through faith in Jesus Christ (*Galatians 3:26*). And if you are Christ's, then you are Abraham's seed, and heirs according to the promise (*Galatians 3:29*). Therefore you are no longer a slave but a son, and if a son, then an heir of God through Christ (*Galatians 4:7*). And we know that the Son of God has come and has given us an understanding, that we may know Him who is true; and we are in Him who is true, in His Son Jesus Christ. This is the true God and eternal life (*1 John 5:20*). "The saints of the Most High shall receive the kingdom, and possess the kingdom forever, even forever and ever" (*Daniel 7:18*). Fear not for I have redeemed you; I have called you by name; you are Mine (*Isaiah 43:1*). Now, therefore you are no longer strangers and foreigners, but fellow citizens with the saints and members of the household of God (*Ephesians 2:19*). He has delivered us from the power of darkness and conveyed us into the kingdom of the Son of His love *(Colossians 1:13)*. Behold what manner of love the Father has bestowed on us, that we should be called children of God (1 John 3:1).

WHOLE HEART FINDS HOLY LORD

And you will seek Me and find Me; when you search for Me with your whole heart (*Jeremiah 29:13*). Blessed are those who keep His testimonies, who seek Him with the whole heart! (*Psalm 119:2*). You are my portion, O Lord; I have said that I would keep Your words. I entreated Your favor with my whole heart; be merciful to me according to Your word (*Psalm 119:58*). Then I will give them a heart to know Me, that I am the LORD; and they shall be My people, and I will be their God, for they shall return to Me with their whole heart (*Jeremiah 24:7*). Again, the kingdom of heaven is like treasure hidden in a field, which a man found and hid; and for joy over it he goes and sells all that he has and buys that field. Again, the kingdom of heaven is like a merchant seeking beautiful pearls, who, when he had found one pearl of great price, went and sold all that he had and bought it (*Matthew 13:44–46*). Blessed are those who hunger and thirst for righteousness, for they shall be filled (*Matthew 5:6*). For You, LORD, have not forsaken those who seek You (*Psalm 9:10*). "All that the Father gives to Me [Jesus] will come to Me, and the one who comes to Me I will by no means cast out *(John 6:37)*."

MAKING TOO MUCH OF MONEY

A faithful man will abound with blessings, but he who hastens to be rich will not go unpunished (*Proverbs 28:20*). But Jesus answered again and said to them, "Children, how hard it is for those who trust in riches to enter the kingdom of God! (*Mark 10:24*). Come to now, you who say, "Today or tomorrow we will go to such and such a city, spend a year there, buy and sell, and make a profit"; whereas you do not know what will happen tomorrow. For what is your life? It is even a vapor that appears for a little time and then vanishes away. Instead you ought to say, "If the Lord wills, we shall live and do this or that" (*James 4:13–15*). But those who desire to be rich fall into temptation and a snare, and into many foolish and harmful lusts which drown men in destruction and perdition. For the love of money is a root of all kinds of evil, for which some have strayed from the faith in their greediness, and pierced themselves through with many sorrows (*1 Timothy 6:9–10*). No one can serve two masters; for he will either hate the one and love the other, or he will be loyal to the one and despise the other. You cannot serve God and mammon [money or greed] (*Matthew 6:24*). "For what profit is it to a man if he gains the whole world, and lose his own soul? Or what will a man give in exchange for his soul? (*Matthew 16:26*). Command those who are rich in this present age not to be haughty, not to trust in uncertain riches but in the living God, who gives us richly all things to enjoy (*1 Timothy 6:17*).

THE LOST VIRTUE OF GENTLENESS

"Take My [Jesus] yoke upon you and learn from Me, for I am gentle and lowly in heart, and you will find rest for your souls. For My yoke is easy and My burden is light" (*Matthew 11:29–30*). A bruised reed He [the Lord Jesus] will not break, and smoking flax He will not quench, till He sends forth justice to victory (*Matthew 12:20*). But we were gentle among you, just as a nursing mother cherishes her own children (*1 Thessalonians 2:7*). And a servant of the Lord must not quarrel but be gentle to all (*2 Timothy 2:24*), to speak evil of no one, to be peaceable, gentle, showing all humility to all men (*Titus 3:2*). But the fruit of the Spirit is love, joy, peace, longsuffering, kindness, goodness, faithfulness, gentleness, self-control. Against such there is no law (*Galatians 5:22–23*). Let your gentleness be known to all men. The Lord is at hand (*Philippians 4:5*). Pursue righteousness, godliness, faith, love, patience, gentleness (*1 Timothy 6:11*). Walk worthy of the calling with which you were called, with all lowliness and gentleness, with longsuffering, bearing with one another in love (*Ephesians 4:1–2*). With the incorruptible beauty of a gentle and quiet spirit, which is very precious in the sight of God (*1 Peter 3:4*). Finally, all of you be of one mind, having compassion for one another; love as brothers, be tenderhearted, be courteous; not returning evil for evil or reviling for reviling, but on the contrary blessing, knowing that you were called to this, that you may inherit a blessing (*1 Peter 3:8–9*).

BABIES KNOW BEST

"I thank You, Father, Lord of heaven and earth, that you have hidden these things from the wise and prudent and have revealed them to babes. Even so, Father, for so it seemed good in Your sight (*Matthew 11:25–26*). And Jesus said to them, "Yes, have you never read, out of the mouth of babes and nursing infants You have perfected praise?" (*Matthew 21:16*). I want you to be wise in what is good and simple concerning evil (*Romans 16:19*). "Blessed are the pure in heart, for they shall see God" (*Matthew 5:8*). "Assuredly, I say to you, unless you are converted and become as little children, you will by no means enter the kingdom of heaven" (*Matthew 18:3*). But Jesus said, "Let the little children come to Me, and do not forbid them; for of such is the kingdom of heaven" (*Matthew 19:14*). May the Lord make you increase and abound in love to one another and to all, just as we do to you, so that He may establish your hearts blameless in holiness before our God and Father at the coming of our Lord Jesus Christ with all His saints (*1 Thessalonians 3:12–13*). Do all things without murmuring and disputing, that you may become blameless and harmless children of God without fault in the midst of a crooked and perverse generation, among whom you shine as lights in the world, holding fast the word of life (*Philippians 2:14–16*).

ARMED WITH THE LORD'S STRENGTH

The LORD God is my strength (*Habakkuk 3:19*). The LORD is the strength of my life (*Psalm 27:1*). Surely in the LORD I have righteousness and strength (*Isaiah 45:24*). Truly I am full of power by the Spirit of the LORD (*Micah 3:8*). For God has not given us a spirit of fear, but of power and of love and of a sound mind (*2 Timothy 1:7*). It is God who arms me with strength, and makes my way perfect (*Psalm 18:32*). God is the strength of my heart and my portion forever (*Psalm 73:26*). "My grace is sufficient for you, for My strength is made perfect in weakness" (*2 Corinthians 12:9*). He gives power to the weak, and to those who have no might He increases strength (*Isaiah 40:29*). Strengthened with all might, according to His glorious power, for all patience and longsuffering with joy; giving thanks to the Father who has qualified us to be partakers of the inheritance of the saints in the light *(Colossians 1:11-12)*. That He would grant you, according to the riches of His glory, to be strengthened with might through His Spirit in the inner man *(Ephesians 3:16)*.

WATCHING OUR WORDS

A lying tongue hates those who are crushed by it, and a flattering mouth works ruin (*Proverbs 26:28*). There is one who speaks like the piercing of a sword, but the tongue of the wise promotes health (*Proverbs 12:18*). My soul is among lions; I lay among the sons of men who are set on fire, whose teeth are spears and arrows, and their tongue a sharp sword (*Psalm 57:4*). You sit and speak against your brother; you slander your own mother's son. These things you have done, and I kept silent; you thought that I was altogether like you; but I will rebuke you, and set them in order before your eyes (*Psalm 50:20–21*). A man who bears false witness against his neighbor is like a club, a sword, and a sharp arrow (*Proverbs 25:18*). He who keeps instruction is in the way of life, but he who refuses correction goes astray. Whoever hides hatred has lying lips, and whoever spreads slander is a fool. In the multitude of words sin is not lacking, but he who restrains his lips is wise (*Proverbs 10:17–19*). "And what shall we do?" So he [John the Baptist] said to them, "Do not intimidate anyone or accuse falsely (*Luke 3:14*). And a servant Lord must not quarrel but be gentle to all, able to teach, patient (*2 Timothy 2:24*), to speak evil of no one, to be peaceable, gentle, showing all humility to all men (*Titus 3:2*). Neither filthiness, nor foolish talking, nor coarse jesting, which are not fitting, but rather giving of thanks. *(Ephesians 5:4)*. But now you yourselves are to put off all these: anger, wrath, malice, blasphemy, filthy language out of your mouth. Do not lie to one another, since you have put off the old man with his deeds, and put on the new man who is renewed in knowledge according to the image of Him who created him (*Colossians 3:8–10*). "But I say to you that every idle word men may speak, they will give an account of it in the day of judgment. For by your words you will be justified, and by your words you will be condemned" (*Matthew 12:36–37*). Put away from you a deceitful mouth, and put perverse lips far from you (*Proverbs 4:24*). Let no corrupt word proceed out of your mouth, but what is good for necessary edification, that it may impart grace to the hearers *(Ephesians 4:29)*. For "He who would love life and see good days, let him refrain his tongue from evil, and his lips from speaking deceit" *(1 Peter 3:10)*. "As many as I love, I rebuke and chasten. Therefore be zealous and repent *(Revelation 3:19)*." Set a guard, O LORD, over my mouth; keep watch over the door of my lips. Do not incline my heart to any evil thing *(Psalm 141:3)*. Watch, stand fast in the faith, be brave, be strong. Let all that you do be done with love (*1 Corinthians 16:13-14*).

HAVING HUMILITY HELPS

A man's pride will bring him low, but the humble will retain honor (*Proverbs 29:23*). By humility and the fear of the LORD are riches and honor and life (*Proverbs 22:4*). For you will save the humble people, but bring down haughty looks (*Psalm 18:27*). People shall be brought down, each man shall be humbled, and the eyes of the lofty shall be humbled (*Isaiah 5:15*), whoever exalts himself will be humbled, and whoever humbles himself will be exalted (*Matthew 23:12*). The humble He guides in justice, and the humble He teaches His way (*Psalm 25:9*). He raises the poor out of the dust, and lifts the needy out of the ash heap, that He may seat him with princes (*Psalm 113:7*). The humble shall increase their joy in the LORD, and the poor among men shall rejoice in the Holy One of Israel (*Isaiah 29:19*). Therefore humble yourselves under the mighty hand of God, that He may exalt you in due time (*1 Peter 5:6*). Humble yourself in the sight of the Lord and He will lift you up (*James 4:10*). You, O LORD, are a shield for me, my glory and the One who lifts my head (*Psalm 3:3*). That, as it is written, "He who glories, let him glory in the LORD" (*1 Corinthians 1:31*).

THE LORD HEARS

Do not hide your face from your servant, for I am in trouble; hear me speedily (*Psalm 69:17*). Hear, O LORD, when I cry with my voice! Have mercy upon me, and answer me. When You said, "Seek my face," my heart said to You, "Your face, LORD, I will seek." Do not hide Your face from me; do not turn Your servant away in anger; You have been my help; do not leave me nor forsake me (*Psalm 27:7–9*). For I said in my haste, "I am cut off from before Your eyes," nevertheless You heard the voice of my supplications when I cried out to You (*Psalm 31:22*). The righteous cry out, and the LORD hears, and delivers them out of all their troubles (*Psalm 34:17*). He hears the prayer of the righteous (*Proverbs 15:29*). For He made Him [Jesus] who knew no sin to be sin for us, that we might become the righteousness of God in Him (*2 Corinthians 5:21*). He [God] has covered me with the robe of righteousness (*Isaiah 61:10*). Then He [Jesus] spoke a parable to them, that men always ought to pray and not lose heart *(Luke 18:1)*. Therefore I will look to the LORD; I will wait for the God of my salvation; my God will hear me (*Micah 7:7*).

LIFE IN HIS LOVING LOOK

He has not despised nor abhorred the affliction of the afflicted; nor has He hidden His face from Him; but when He cried to Him, He heard *(Psalm 22:24)*. "For the LORD your God is gracious and merciful, and will not turn His face from you if you return to Him" *(2 Chronicles 30:9)*. The LORD is righteous, He loves righteousness; His countenance beholds the upright *(Psalm 11:7)*. Make Your face shine upon Your servant, and teach me Your statutes *(Psalm 119:135)*. I have set the LORD always before me; because He is at my right hand I shall not be moved. Therefore my heart is glad, and my glory rejoices; my flesh also will rest in hope *(Psalm 16:8–9)*. The LORD bless you and keep you; the LORD make His face shine upon you, and be gracious to you; the LORD lift up His countenance upon you, and give you peace *(Numbers 6:24–26)*. God be merciful to us and bless us, and cause His face to shine upon us, that Your way may be known on earth, Your salvation among all nations *(Psalm 67:1–2)*. LORD, lift up the light of Your countenance upon us *(Psalm 4:6)*. Make Your face shine upon Your servant; save me for Your mercies sake *(Psalm 31:16)*. Turn us back to You, O LORD, and we will be restored; renew our days as of old *(Lamentations 5:21)*. Righteousness and justice are the foundation of Your throne; mercy and truth go before Your face. Blessed are the people who know the joyful sound! They walk, O LORD, in the light of Your countenance. In Your name they rejoice all day long, and in Your righteousness they are exalted. For You are the glory of their strength, and in Your favor our horn is exalted. For our shield belongs to the LORD *(Psalm 89:14-18)*. For they did not gain possession of the land by their own sword, nor did their own arm save them; but it was Your right arm, and the light of Your countenance, because You favored them *(Psalm 44:3)*. Seek the LORD and His strength; seek His face evermore *(Psalm 105:4)!* He [Jesus] was transfigured before them. His face shone like the sun, and His clothes became as white as light *(Matthew 17:2)*. For it is the God who commanded light to shine out of darkness, who has shone in our hearts to give the light of the knowledge of the glory of God in the face of Jesus Christ *(2 Corinthians 4:6)*. Restore us, O God; cause Your face to shine, and we shall be saved! (*Psalm 80:3*).

DAY BY DAY IS GOD'S WAY

I will sing praise to Your name forever, that I may daily perform my vows *(Psalm 61:8)*. The people shall go out and gather a certain quota [of manna] every day, that I may test them, whether they will walk in My law or not *(Exodus 16:4)*. Give us this day our daily bread *(Matthew 6:11)*. And as for his provisions, there was a regular ration given him by the king, a portion for each day, all the days of his life *(2 Kings 25:30)*, sufficient unto the day is its own trouble *(Matthew 6:34)*. As your days, so shall your strength be *(Deuteronomy 33:25)*. Blessed be the Lord, who daily loads us with benefits, the God of our salvation! *(Psalm 68:19)*. Then He said to them all, "If anyone desires to come after Me, let Him deny himself, and take up His cross daily and follow Me" *(Luke 9:23)*. We do not lose heart, even though our outward man is perishing, yet the inward man is being renewed day by day *(2 Corinthians 4:16)*. "Choose for yourselves this day whom you will serve. But as for me and my house, we will serve the LORD *(Joshua 24:15)*." From the rising of the sun to its going down the LORD'S name is to be praised *(Psalm 113:3)*. This is the day the LORD has made; we will rejoice and be glad in it *(Psalm 118:24)*. Today, if you will hear His voice, do not harden your hearts *(Psalm 113:3 and Hebrews 4:7)*. Behold, now is the accepted time; behold now is the day of salvation *(2 Corinthians 6:2)*.

AVOIDING ANXIETY

"Peace I [Jesus] leave with you, My peace I give to you; not as the world gives do I give to you. Let not your heart be troubled, neither let it be afraid" (*John 14:27*), nor have an anxious mind (*Luke 12:29*). Anxiety in the heart of man causes depression, but a good word makes it glad (*Proverbs 12:25*). Be anxious for nothing, but in everything by prayer and supplication, with thanksgiving, let your requests be made known to God: and the peace of God, which surpasses all understanding, will guard your hearts and minds through Christ Jesus (*Philippians 4:6–7*), casting all your care upon Him, for He cares for you (*1 Peter 5:7*). Cast your burden on the LORD, and He shall sustain you; He shall never permit the righteous to be moved (*Psalm 55:22*). In the multitude of my anxieties within me, Your comforts delight my soul (*Psalm 94:19*). Trust in the LORD, and do good; dwell in the land, and feed on His faithfulness *(Psalm 37:3)*. You will keep him in perfect peace whose mind is stayed on You *(Isaiah 26:3)*.

FRUITFUL WITH OUR LIPS

Blessed be God, who has not turned away my prayer, nor His mercy from me! (*Psalm 66:20*). Blessed be the LORD, because He heard the voice of my supplications! (*Psalm 28:6*). I will greatly praise the LORD with my mouth; yes, I will praise Him among the multitude (*Psalm 109:30*). Because Your loving-kindness is better than life, my lips shall praise You (*Psalm 63:3*). My soul shall be satisfied as with marrow and fatness, and my mouth shall praise You with joyful lips (*Psalm 63:5*). Therefore by Him let us continually offer the sacrifice of praise to God, that is, the fruit of our lips, giving thanks to His name (*Hebrews 13:15*). Praise the LORD! Oh, give thanks to the LORD, for He is good! For His mercy endures forever (*Psalm 106:1*). It is good to give thanks to the LORD, and to sing praises to Your name, O Most High; to declare Your loving-kindness in the morning, and Your faithfulness every night (*Psalm 92:1–2*).

ASSESSABLE AFFIRMATION

That we should no longer be children, tossed to and fro and carried about with every wind of doctrine, by the trickery of men, in the cunning craftiness of deceitful plotting (*Ephesians 4:14*). "If anyone wills to do His [God the Father's] will, he shall know concerning the doctrine, whether it is from God or whether I [Jesus] speak on my own authority" (*John 7:17*). By this we know that we are in Him, and He in us, because He has given us of His Spirit (*1 John 4:13*). Now hope does not disappoint, because the love of God has been poured out in our hearts by the Holy Spirit who has been given to us (*Romans 5:5*). The Spirit Himself bears witness with our spirit that we are children of God (*Romans 8:16*). He who believes in the Son of God has the witness in Himself (*1 John 5:10*). "All that the Father gives to Me [Jesus] will come to me, and the one who comes to Me I will by no means cast out" (*John 6:37*). He who abides in the doctrine of Christ has both the Father and Son (*2 John 1:9*). Whoever denies the Son does not have the Father either; he who acknowledges the Son has the Father also. Therefore let that abide in you which you heard from the beginning. If what you heard from the beginning abides in you, you also will abide in the Son and in the Father. And this is the promise that He has promised us—eternal life (*1 John 3:23–25*). Truly our fellowship is with the Father and His Son Jesus Christ (*1 John 1:3*). And this is the testimony that God has given us eternal life, and this life is in His Son [Jesus Christ]. He who has the Son has life; he who does not have the Son of God does not have life. These things I have written to you who believe in the name of the Son of God, that you may know that you have eternal life, and that you may continue to believe in the name of the Son of God (*1 John 5:11–13*). Moreover whom He predestined, these He also called; whom He called; these He also justified; and whom He justified; these He also glorified *(Romans 8:30)*. God is faithful, by whom you were called into fellowship of His Son, Jesus Christ our Lord *(1 Corinthians 1:9)*. Being confident of this very thing, that He who has begun a good work in you will complete it until the day of Jesus Christ *(Philippians 1:6)*. Let us hold fast the confession of our hope without wavering, for He who promised is faithful *(Hebrews 10:23)*.

CORRECTED, NOT CONDEMNED

It is good for me that I have been afflicted, that I may learn Your statutes (*Psalm 119:71*). And have you forgotten the exhortation which speaks to you as to sons: "My son, do not despise the chastening of the LORD, nor be discouraged when you are rebuked by Him; for whom the LORD loves He chastens, and scourges every son whom He receives." If you endure chastening, God deals with you as with sons; for what son is there whom a father does not chasten? But if you are without chastening, of which all have become partakers, then you are illegitimate and not sons. Furthermore, we have had human fathers who corrected us, and we paid them respect. Shall we not much more readily be in subjection to the Father of spirits and live? For they indeed for a few days chastened us as seemed best to them, but He for our profit, that we may be partakers of His holiness. Now no chastening seems to be joyful for the present, but painful; nevertheless, afterward it yields the peaceable fruit of righteousness to those who have been trained by it (*Hebrews 12:5–11*). My son, do not despise the chastening of the LORD, for whom the LORD loves He corrects, just as a father the son in whom he delights (*Proverbs 3:11–12*). But when we are judged, we are chastened by the Lord, that we may not be condemned with the world (*1 Corinthians 11:32*). Behold, happy is the man whom God corrects; therefore do not despise the chastening of the Almighty. For He bruises, but He binds up; He wounds, but His hands make whole (*Job 5:17–18*).

TRADING TRAUMA FOR DOUBLE HONOR

Oh, that my ways were directed to keep Your statutes! Then I would not be ashamed (*Psalm 119:5–6*). "Behold, at that time I will deal with all who afflict you; I will save the lame, and gather those who were driven out; I will appoint them for praise and fame in every land where they were put to shame" (*Zephaniah 3:19*). But as it is written: "Eye has not seen, nor ear heard, nor have entered into the heart of man the things which God has prepared for those who love Him" (*1 Corinthians 2:19*). *"*Blessed are those who are persecuted for righteousness' sake, for theirs is the kingdom of heaven. Blessed are you when they revile and persecute you, and say all kinds of evil against you falsely for My sake. Rejoice and be exceedingly glad, for great is your reward in heaven, for so they persecuted the prophets who were before you *(Matthew 5:10-12)."* For to you it has been granted on behalf of Christ, not only to believe in Him, but also to suffer for His sake *(Philippians 1:29)*. The Spirit Himself bears witness with our spirit that we are children of God, and if children, then heirs—heirs of God and joint heir with Christ, if indeed we suffer with Him, that we may also be glorified together. For I consider that the sufferings of this present time are not worthy to be compared with the glory which shall be revealed in us *(Romans 8:16-18)*. Instead of your shame you shall have double honor, and instead of confusion they shall rejoice in their portion. Therefore in their land they shall possess double; everlasting joy shall be theirs. For I the LORD love justice (*Isaiah 61:7–8*).

FULLY FORGIVEN FOREVER

Who is a God like You, pardoning iniquity and passing over the transgression of the remnant of His heritage? He does not retain His anger forever, because He delights in mercy. He will again have compassion on us, and subdue our iniquities. You will cast all our sins into the depths of the sea (*Micah 7:18–19*). If we confess our sins, He is faithful and just to forgive us our sins and to cleanse us from all unrighteousness (*1 John 1:9*). "To Him [Jesus Christ] all the prophets witness that, through His name, whoever believes in Him will receive remission of sins" (*Acts 10:42–43*). In Him [Jesus] we have redemption through His blood, the forgiveness of sins according to the riches of His grace (*Ephesians 1:7*). And you, being dead in your trespasses and the uncircumcision of your flesh, He [God] has made alive together with Him [Jesus] having forgiven you all trespasses, having wiped out the handwriting of requirements that was against us, which was contrary to us. And He has taken it out of the way, having nailed it to the cross *(Colossians 2:13-14)*. That having been justified by His grace we should become heirs according to the hope of eternal life (*Titus 3:7*). "I have blotted out, like a thick cloud, your transgressions, and like a cloud, your sins. Return to Me, for I have redeemed you" (*Isaiah 44:22*). So great is His mercy toward those who fear Him; as far as the east is from the west, so far has He removed our transgressions from us. As a father pities his children, so the LORD pities those who fear Him. For He knows our frame; He remembers that we are dust (*Psalm 103:11–14*), who once were not a people but are now the people of God, who had not obtained mercy but now have obtained mercy (*1 Peter 2:10*). By that will [God's] we have been sanctified through the offering of the body of Jesus Christ once for all *(Hebrews 10:10)*.

GOD'S GRACIOUS GUIDANCE

As many as are led by the Spirit of God, these are the sons of God. For you did not receive the spirit of bondage again to fear, but you received the Spirit of adoption by whom we cry out, "Abba, Father" *(Romans 8:14-15)*. Lead me and guide me *(Psalm 31:3)*. Teach me to do Your will, for You are my God; Your Spirit is good. Lead me in the land of uprightness *(Psalm 143:10)*. The LORD of Hosts, who is wonderful in counsel and excellent in guidance *(Isaiah 28:29)*. Wonderful counselor, mighty God *(Isaiah 9:6)*, I will instruct you and teach you in the way you should go; I will guide you with My eye. Do not be like the horse or like the mule, which have no understanding, which must be harnessed with bit and bridle, else they will not come near you [not praying or seeking godly counsel] *(Psalm 32:8–9)*. So He shepherded them according to the integrity of His heart, and guided them by the skillfulness of His hands *(Psalm 78:72)*. Your testimonies also are my delight and my counselors *(Psalm 119:24)*. To be guided continually, see *Isaiah 58*. We are His workmanship, created in Christ Jesus for good works, which God prepared beforehand that we should walk in them *(Ephesians 2:10)*. I am the vine, you are the branches. He who abides in Me, and I in him, bears much fruit; for without Me you can do nothing *(John 15:5)*. Let us lay aside every weight, and the sin which so easily ensnares us, and let us run with endurance the race that is set before us, looking unto Jesus, the author and finisher of our faith *(Hebrews 12:1-2)*. Therefore we make it our aim to be well pleasing to Him *(2 Corinthians 5:9)*. And do not be conformed to this world, but be transformed by the renewing of your mind, that you may prove what is that good and acceptable and perfect will of God *(Romans 12:2)*. Even to your old age, I am He, and even to gray hairs I will carry you! I have made, and I will bear;

even I will carry you, and will deliver you *(Isaiah 46:4)*. For this is God, our God forever and ever; He will be our guide even to death (*Psalm 48:14*). You will guide me with Your counsel, and afterward receive me to glory (*Psalm 73:24*).

PRESERVED TO BE PRESENTED FAULTLESS

O love the LORD, all you His saints: for the LORD preserves the faithful (*Psalm 31:23*). To those who are called, sanctified by God the Father, and preserved in Jesus Christ; mercy, peace and love be multiplied you, beloved (*Jude 1:2–3*). Blessed be the God and Father of our Lord Jesus Christ, who according to His abundant mercy has begotten us again to a living hope through the resurrection of Jesus Christ from the dead, to an inheritance incorruptible and undefiled and that does not fade away, reserved in heaven for you, who are kept by the power of God through faith for salvation ready to be revealed in the last time (*1 Peter 1:3–5*). Now to Him who is able to keep you from stumbling, and present you faultless before the presence of His glory with exceeding joy, to God our Savior, who alone is wise, be glory and majesty, dominion and power, both now and forever. Amen (*Jude 1:24–25*).

CHOOSING WISDOM OVER WEALTH

There is no wisdom or understanding or counsel against the LORD (*Proverbs 21:30*). Light is sown for the righteous (*Psalm 97:11*). The fear of the LORD [to delight greatly in His commandments] is the beginning of wisdom, and knowledge of the Holy One is understanding. For by me your days will be multiplied, and years of life will be added to you. If you are wise, you are wise for yourself, and if you scoff [mock at doing right] you will bear it (*Proverbs 9:10–12*). How much better to get wisdom than gold! And understanding is to be chosen rather than silver (*Proverbs 16:16*). Happy is the man who finds wisdom, and the man who gains understanding; for her proceeds are better than the profits of silver, and her gain than fine gold. She is more precious than rubies, and all the things you may desire cannot be compare with her. Length of days is in her right hand, in her left hand riches and honor. Her ways are ways of pleasantness, and all her paths are peace. She is a tree of life to those who take hold of her, and happy are all who retain her (*Proverbs 3:13–18*). He who gets wisdom loves his own soul; he who keeps understanding will find good (*Proverbs 19:8*). Take firm hold of instruction, do not let go; keep her, for she is your life (*Proverbs 4:13*). My son, eat honey because it is good, and the honeycomb which is sweet to your taste; so shall the knowledge of wisdom be to your soul; if you have found it, there is a prospect, and your hope will not be cut off (*Proverbs 24:14*). If any of you lacks wisdom, let him ask of God, who gives to all liberally and without reproach, and it will be given to him (*James 1:5*).

POOR PLAN TO TRUST IN MAN

Woe to those who go down to Egypt [stop seeking God] for help,...but do not look to the Holy One of Israel, nor seek the LORD! (*Isaiah 31:1*). For the LORD has rejected your trusted allies, and you will not prosper by them (*Jeremiah 2:37*). Do not put your trust in princes, nor in a son of man, in whom there is no help. His spirit departs, he returns to the earth; in that day his plans perish (*Psalm 146 3:4*). It is better to trust in the LORD than to put confidence in man (*Psalm 118:8*). The fear of man brings a snare, but whoever trusts in the LORD shall be safe (*Proverbs 25:29*). O LORD of Hosts, blessed is the man who trusts in You! (*Psalm 84:12*). But as for me, I will trust in You, O LORD; I will say, "You are my God." My times are in Your hands (*Psalm 31:14–15*). I will say of the LORD, "He is my refuge and my fortress; my God, in Him I trust" (*Psalm 91:2*). "Let not your heart be troubled; you believe in God, believe also in me (Jesus Christ)" (*John 14:1*). So we may boldly say: "The LORD is my helper; I will not fear. What can man do to me?" (*Hebrews 13:6*). God is faithful, by whom you were called into the fellowship of His Son, Jesus Christ out Lord (*1 Corinthians 1:9*). For all the promises of God in Him are Yes, and in Him Amen, to the glory of God through us *(2 Corinthians 1:20).*

THE LAZY LOSE

Do not love sleep, lest you come to poverty; open your eyes, and you will be satisfied with bread (*Proverbs 20:13*). Laziness casts one into a deep sleep, and an idle person will suffer hunger (*Proverbs 19:13*). The lazy man does not roast what he took in hunting, but diligence is man's precious possession (*Proverbs 12:27*). He who tills His land will be satisfied with bread (*Proverbs 12:11*). He who tills his land will have plenty of bread, but he who follows frivolity will have poverty enough! (*Proverbs 28:19*). He who has a slack hand becomes poor, but the hand diligent makes rich. He who gathers in summer is a wise son; he who sleeps in harvest is a son who causes shame (*Proverbs 10:4–5*). Because of laziness the building decays, and through idleness of hands the house leaks *(Ecclesiastes 10:18)*. The soul of a lazy man desires and has nothing; but the diligent shall be made rich (*Proverbs 13:4*). I went by the field of the lazy man, and by the vineyard of the man devoid of understanding; and there it was, all overgrown with thorns; its surface was covered with nettles; its stone wall was broken down. When I saw it, I considered it well; I looked on it and received instruction: A little sleep, a little slumber, a little folding of the hands to rest; so shall your poverty come like a prowler, and your need like an armed man (*Proverbs 24:30–34*).

FROM TEARS TO TRIUMPH

Those who sow in tears shall reap in joy. He who continually goes forth weeping, bearing seed for sowing, shall doubtless come again with rejoicing, bringing his sheaves with him (*Psalm 126:5–6*). We are hard pressed on every side, yet not crushed; we are perplexed, but not in despair; persecuted, but not forsaken; struck down, but not destroyed—always carrying about in the body the dying of the Lord Jesus, that the life of Jesus also may be manifested in our body (*2 Corinthians 4:8–10*). For our light affliction, which is but for a moment, is working for us a far more exceeding and eternal weight of glory (*2 Corinthians 4:17*). The ransomed of the Lord shall return, and come to Zion with singing, with everlasting joy on their heads. They shall obtain joy and gladness, and sorrow and sighing shall flee away (*Isaiah 35:10*). Most assuredly, I say to you that you will weep and lament, but the world will rejoice; and you will be sorrowful, but your sorrow will be turned into joy. A woman, when she is in labor, has sorrow because her hour has come; but as soon as she has given birth to the child, she no longer remains in anguish, for the joy that a human being has been born into the world. "Therefore you now have sorrow; but I will see you again and your heart shall rejoice, and your joy no one will take from you. And in that day you will ask Me nothing. Most assuredly, I say to you, whatever you ask the Father in My name He will give you. Until now you have asked nothing in My name. Ask, and you will receive, that your joy may be full" (*John 16:20–24*). Now thanks be to God who always leads us in triumph in Christ, and through us diffuses the fragrance of His knowledge in every place (*2 Corinthians 2:14*).

MINDING OUR OWN MATTERS

That you also aspire to live a quiet life, to mind your own business and to work with your own hands, as we commanded you, that you walk properly toward those who are outside, and that you may lack nothing (*1 Thessalonians 4:11–12*). Let none of you suffer as a murderer, a thief, an evildoer, or as a busybody in other people's matters (*1 Peter 4:15*). For we hear that there are some who walk among you in a disorderly manner, not working at all, but are busybodies. Now those who are such we command and exhort through our Lord Jesus Christ that they work in quietness and eat their own bread (*2 Thessalonians 3:11–12*). But let each one examine his own work, and then he will have rejoicing in himself alone, and not in another (*Galatians 6:4*). And whatever you do, do it heartily, as to the Lord and not to men, knowing that from the Lord you will receive the reward of the inheritance; for you serve the Lord Christ (*Colossians 3:23–24*).

OUR PRECIOUS PRIEST

But Christ came as High Priest of the good things to come, with the greater and more perfect tabernacle [place of worship] not made with hands, that is not of this creation *(Hebrews 9:11)*. Therefore, in all things He had to be made like His brethren, that He might be a merciful and faithful High Priest in things pertaining to God, to make propitiation for the sins of the people. For in that He Himself has suffered, being tempted, He is able to aid those who are tempted *(Hebrews 2:17-18)*. He [Jesus] because He continues forever, has an unchangeable priesthood. Therefore He is also able to save to the uttermost those who come to God through Him, since He always lives to make intercession for them *(Hebrews 7:24–25)*. Seeing then that we have a great high priest who has passed through the heavens, Jesus the Son of God, let us hold fast our confession. For we do not have a high priest who cannot sympathize with our weaknesses, but was in all points tempted as we are, yet without sin. Let us therefore come boldly to the throne of grace, that we may obtain mercy, and find grace to help in time of need *(Hebrews 4:14–16)*. Now this is the main point of the things we are saying: We have such a High Priest, who is seated at the right hand of the throne of the Majesty in the heavens *(Hebrews 8:1)*.

PROVIDING THE POOR WITH PLENTY

They [the apostles in Jerusalem] desired only that we [Paul, Barnabas, and Titus] should remember the poor, the very thing which I [Paul] also was eager to do (*Galatians 2:10*). You have the poor with you always, and whenever you wish you may do them good (*Mark 14:7*). The righteous considers the cause of the poor (*Proverbs 29:7*). The righteous shows mercy and gives (*Psalm 37:21*). He who has a generous eye will be blessed, for he gives his bread to the poor (*Proverbs 22:9*). He who oppresses the poor reproaches his maker, but he who honors Him has mercy on the needy (*Proverbs 14:31*). He who has pity on the poor lends to the LORD, and He will pay back what he has given (*Proverbs 19:17*). He who gives to the poor will not lack (*Proverbs 28:27*). He who has mercy on the poor, happy is he (*Proverbs 14:21*). For the poor will never cease from the land; therefore I command you, saying, "You shall open your hand wide to your brother, to your poor and your needy, in the land" (*Deuteronomy 15:11*).

WONDERFUL IF WE'D WALK IN HIS WAYS

"But this is what I commanded them, saying, 'Obey My voice, and I will be your God, and you shall be My people. And walk in all the ways that I commanded you, that it may be well with you'" (*Jeremiah 7:23*). "So if you walk in My ways, to keep My statutes and My commandments, as your father David walked, then I will lengthen your days" (*1 Kings 3:14*). Oh, that My people would listen to Me, that Israel would walk in my ways! I would soon subdue their enemies, and turn My hand against their adversaries (*Psalm 81:13–14*). As for God, His way is perfect; the word of the LORD is proven; He is a shield to all who trust in Him (*Psalm 18:30*). For as the heavens are higher than the earth, so My ways are higher than your ways, and My thoughts are higher than your thoughts (*Isaiah 55:9*). The way of the LORD is strength for the upright, but destruction will come to the workers of iniquity (*Proverbs 10:29*). Whoever walks blamelessly will be saved, but he who is perverse in his ways will suddenly fall (*Proverbs 28:18*). Thus says the LORD: "Stand in the ways and see, and ask for the old paths, where the good way is, and walk in it; then you will find rest for your souls (*Jeremiah 6:16*). Blessed is everyone who fears the LORD, who walks in His ways (*Psalm 128:1*). He who walks with integrity walks securely, but he who perverts his ways will become know (*Proverbs 10:9*). Who is wise? Let him understand these things. Who is prudent? Let him know them. For the ways of the LORD are right; the righteous walk in them, but transgressors stumble in them (*Hosea 14:9*). He who loves his brother abides in the light, and there is no cause for stumbling in him (*1 John 2:10*). Now to Him who is able to keep you from stumbling, and to present you faultless before the presence of His glory with exceeding joy. To God our Savior, Who alone is wise, be majesty, dominion and power, both now and forever. Amen (*Jude 1:24-25*).

LETTING HIS PEACE RULE

"There is no peace," says the LORD, "for the wicked" (*Isaiah 48:22*). Oh, that you had heeded My commands! Then your peace would have been like a river (*Isaiah 48:18*). Mark the blameless man, and observe the upright; for the future of that man is peace (*Psalm 37:37*). The work of righteousness will be peace, and the effect of righteousness, quietness and assurance forever (*Isaiah 32:17*). Now the fruit of righteousness is sown in peace by those who make peace (*James 3:18*). Be at peace among yourselves (*1 Thessalonians 5:13*). Endeavoring to keep the unity of the Spirit in the bond of peace (*Ephesians 4:3*). To speak evil of no one, to be peaceable, gentle, showing all humility to all men (*Titus 3:2*). And let the peace of God rule in your hearts, to which also you were called in one body, and be thankful (*Colossians 3:15*). If possible, as much as depends on you, live peaceably with all men (*Romans 12:18*). Finally, brethren, whatever things are true, whatever things are noble, whatever things are just, whatever things are pure, whatever things are lovely, whatever things are of good report, if there is any virtue and if there is anything praise worthy—meditate on these things. The things which you learned and received and heard and saw in me, [the apostle Paul] these do, and the God of peace will be with you (*Philippians 4:8–9*). Become complete. Be of good comfort, be of one mind, live in peace; and the God of love and peace will be with you (*2 Corinthians 13:11*). Be anxious for nothing, but in everything by prayer and supplication, with thanksgiving, let your requests be made to God; and the peace of God, which surpasses all understanding, will guard your hearts and minds through Christ Jesus (*Philippians 4:6–7*). You will keep him in perfect peace, whose mind is stayed on You, because he trusts in You (*Isaiah 26:3*). Now may the Lord of peace Himself give you peace always in every way. The Lord be with you all (*2 Thessalonians 3:16*).

NOT LAW OR WORKS, BUT GRACE THROUGH FAITH

I live by faith in the Son of God [Jesus]; who loved me and gave Himself for me. I do not set aside the grace of God; for if righteousness comes through the law, then Christ died in vain (*Galatians 2:20–21*). "Knowing that a man is not justified by the works of the law but by faith in Jesus Christ" (*Galatians 2:16*). But when the kindness and the love of God our Savior toward man appeared, not by works of righteousness which we have done, but according to His mercy He saved us, through the washing of regeneration and the renewing of the Holy Spirit, whom He poured out on us abundantly through Jesus Christ our Savior, that having been justified by His grace we should become heirs according to the hope of eternal life (*Titus 3:4–7*). To him who does not work but believes on Him who justifies the ungodly, his faith is accounted for righteousness (*Romans 4:5*). But now the righteousness of God apart from the law is revealed, being witnessed by the law and the prophets, even the righteousness of God, through faith in Jesus Christ, to all and on all who believe. For there is no difference, for all have sinned and fall short of the glory of God, being justified freely by His grace through the redemption that is in Christ Jesus (*Romans 3:21–24*). For the law of the Spirit of life in Christ Jesus has made me free from the law of sin and death (*Romans 8:2*). For Christ is the end of the law for righteousness to everyone who believes (*Romans 10:4*). Therefore, having been justified by faith, we have peace with God through our Lord Jesus Christ, through whom also we have access by faith into this grace in which we stand, and rejoice in hope of the glory of God (*Romans 5:1–2*). Who [God] saved us and called us with a holy calling, not according to our works, but according to His own purpose and grace which was given to us in Christ Jesus before time began, but has now been revealed by the appearing of our Savior Jesus Christ, who has abolished death and brought life and immortality to light through the gospel (*2 Timothy 1:9–10*).

OUR SAVING SHIELD

He stores up sound wisdom for the upright; He is a shield to those who walk uprightly. He guards the paths of justice, and preserves the way of His saints *(Proverbs 2:7–8)*. You, O LORD will bless the righteous; with favor You will surround him as with a shield *(Psalm 5:12)*. Every word of God is pure; He is a shield to those who put their trust in Him *(Proverbs 30:5)*. As for God, His way is perfect; the word of the LORD is proven; He is a shield to all who trust in Him *(Psalm 18:30)*. You who fear the LORD, trust in the LORD; He is their help and their shield *(Psalm 115:11)*. "Do not be afraid, Abram. I am your shield, your exceedingly great reward" *(Genesis 15:1)*. Our soul waits for the LORD; He is our help and our shield *(Psalm 33:20)*. But You, O LORD, are a shield for me, my glory and the One who lifts up my head *(Psalm 3:3)*. The LORD is my strength and my shield; my heart trusted in Him, and I am helped; therefore my heart greatly rejoices, and with my song I will praise Him *(Psalm 28:7)*. Above all, taking the shield of faith with which you will be able to quench all the fiery darts of the wicked one *(Ephesians 6:16)*.

COURAGEOUS, FOR YOU ARE WITH US

"Have I not commanded you? Be strong and of a good courage; do not be afraid, nor dismayed, for the LORD your God is with you wherever you go" (*Joshua 1:9*). Yea, though I walk through the valley of the shadow of death, I will fear no evil; for you are with me (*Psalm 23:4*). When you pass through the waters, I will be with you; and through the rivers, they shall not overflow you (*Isaiah 43:2*). You shall not be terrified of them; for the LORD your God, the great and awesome God, is among you (*Deuteronomy 7:21*). Fear not, for I am with you; be not dismayed, for I am your God. I will strengthen you, yes, I will help you, I will uphold you with My righteous right hand (*Isaiah 41:10*). God is our refuge and strength, a very present help in time trouble. Therefore we will not fear, even though the earth be removed, and though the mountains be carried into the midst of the sea; though its waters roar and be troubled, though the mountains shake with its swelling (*Psalm 46:1–3*). I can do all things [including being courageous] through Christ who strengthens me (*Philippians 4:13*). And lo, I [Christ] am with you always, even to the end of the age." Amen (*Matthew 28:20*). And the LORD, He is the One who goes before you. He will be with you. He will not leave you nor forsake you; do not fear nor be dismayed (*Deuteronomy 31:8*). Let all that you do be done with love *(1 Corinthians 16:14)*. There is no fear in love; but perfect love casts out fear *(1 John 4:18)*. For God has not given us a spirit of fear, but of power and of love and of a sound mind *(2 Timothy 1:7)*.

WALKING HUMBLY WITH YOUR GOD

He who is of a proud heart stirs up strife, but he who trusts in the LORD will be prospered (*Proverbs 28:25*). Speak evil of no one, to be peaceable, gentle, showing all humility to all men (*Titus 3:1*). By pride comes nothing but strife, but with the well advised is wisdom (*Proverbs 13:10*). He who loves transgression loves strife, and he who exalts his gate seeks destruction (*Proverbs 17:19*). If you have been foolish in exalting yourself or if you have devised evil, put your hand on your mouth (*Proverbs 30:32*). He has shown you, O man, what is good; and what does the LORD require of you but to do justly, to love mercy, and walk humbly with your God? (*Micah 6:8*). Let another man praise you, and not your own mouth; a stranger, and not your own lips (*Proverbs 27:2*). It is not good to eat much honey, so to seek one's own glory is not glory (*Proverbs 25:27*). Thus says the LORD: "Let not the wise man glory in his wisdom, let not the mighty man glory in his might, nor let the rich man glory in his riches; but let him who glories glory in this, that he understands and knows Me, that I am the LORD, exercising lovingkindness, judgment, and righteousness in the earth. For in these things I delight," says the LORD (*Jeremiah 9:23-24*).

A HEAVENLY HUG

He will quiet you with His love *(Zephaniah 3:17)*. "For I have satiated the weary soul, and I have replenished every sorrowful soul" *(Jeremiah 31:25)*. To comfort all who mourn, to console those who mourn in Zion, to giving them beauty for ashes, the oil of joy for mourning, the garment of praise for the spirit of heaviness *(Isaiah 61:2–3)*. The eternal God is your refuge, and underneath are everlasting arms *(Deuteronomy 33:27)*. As one whom his mother comforts, so I will comfort you *(Isaiah 66:13)*. "Yes, I have loved you with an everlasting love; therefore with loving-kindness I have drawn you" *(Jeremiah 31:3)*. But God who is rich in mercy, because of His great love with which He loved us, even when we were dead in trespasses, made us alive together with Christ [by grace you have been saved] *(Ephesians 2:4–5)*. Now may our Lord Jesus Christ Himself, and our God and Father, who has loved us and given us everlasting consolation and good hope by grace, comfort your hearts and establish you in every good word and work *(2 Thessalonians 2:16–17)*

FAITH IN CHRIST BRINGS AND KEEPS LIFE

Whoever transgresses and does not abide in the doctrine of Christ does not have God. He who abides in the doctrine of Christ has both the Father and the Son (*2 John 1:9*). Therefore let that abide in you which you heard from the beginning. If what you heard from the beginning abides in you, you also will abide in the Son and in the Father. And this is the promise that He has promised us—eternal life (*1 John 2:24–25*). The eyes of the LORD run to and fro throughout the whole earth, to show Himself strong on behalf of those whose heart is loyal to Him (*2 Chronicles 16:9*). My sheep hear My voice, and I know them, and they follow Me. And I give them eternal life, and they shall never perish; neither shall anyone snatch them out of My hand. My Father who has given them to Me, is greater than all; and no one is able to snatch them out of My Father's hand. I and My Father are one (*John 10:27–30*). But we are bound to give thanks to God always for you, brethren beloved by the Lord, because God from the beginning chose you for salvation through sanctification by the Spirit and belief in the truth, to which He called you by our gospel, for the obtaining of the glory of our Lord Jesus Christ. Therefore, brethren, stand fast and hold the traditions which you were taught, whether by word or epistle (*2 Thessalonians 2:13–15*). Blessed be the God and Father of our Lord Jesus Christ, who according to His abundant mercy has begotten us again to a living hope through the resurrection of Jesus Christ from the dead, to an inheritance incorruptible and undefiled and does not fade away, reserved in heaven for you, who are kept by the power of God through faith for salvation ready to be revealed in the last time (*1 Peter 1:3-5*).

THE WORD DOES GOOD

Laying aside all malice, all deceit, hypocrisy, envy, and all evil speaking, as new born babes, desire the pure milk of the word, that you may grow thereby, if indeed you have tasted that the Lord is gracious *(1 Peter 2:1-3)*. For whatever things were written before were written for our learning, that we through the patience and comfort of Scriptures might have hope (*Romans 15:4*). For the ways of the LORD are right, the righteous walk in them, but transgressors stumble in them (*Hosea 14:9*). Do not my words do good to him who walks uprightly? (*Micah 2:7*). All Scripture is given by inspiration of God, and is profitable for doctrine, for reproof, for correction, for instruction in righteousness, that the man of God may be completely equipped for every good work (*2 Timothy 3:16–17*). Take heed to yourself and to the doctrine. Continue in them, for in doing this you will save both yourself and those who hear you (*1 Timothy 4:16*). And now, brethren, I commend you to God and to the word of His grace, which is able to build you up and give you an inheritance among those who are being sanctified [set aside for holiness] (*Acts 20:32*). Having been born again, not of corruptible seed but incorruptible, through the word of God which lives and abides forever *(1 Peter 1:23)*.

LOVING BRINGS ASSURANCE

Since you have purified your souls in obeying the truth through the Spirit in sincere love of the brethren, love one another fervently with a pure heart, having been born again, not of corruptible seed but incorruptible, through the word of God which lives and abides forever (*1 Peter 1:22–23*). We know that we have passed from death to life, because we love the brethren (*1 John 3:14*). For all the law is fulfilled in one word, even in this: "You shall love your neighbor as yourself" (*Galatians 5:14*). If you really fulfill the royal law according to the scripture, "You shall love your neighbor as yourself," you do well (*James 2:8*). Love has been perfected among us in this: that we may have boldness in the day of judgment; because as He is, so are we in the world (*1 John 4:17*). And this commandment we have from Him: that He who loves God must love his brother also *(1 John 4:21)*. By this we know that we love the children of God, when we love God and keep His commandments [to love God and our neighbor as ourselves]. For this is the love of God, that we keep His commandments. And His commandments are not burdensome (*1 John 5:2*). Let us not love in word or in tongue, but in deed and truth. And by this we know that we are of the truth, and shall assure our hearts before Him (*1 John 3:18–19*). Therefore, whatever you want men to do to you, do also to them, for this is the Law and the Prophets (*Matthew 7:12*). He who loves his brother abides in the light, and there is no cause for stumbling in him (*1 John 2:10*). Finally, all of you be of one mind, having compassion for one another; love as brothers, be tenderhearted, be courteous; not returning evil for evil or reviling for reviling, but on the contrary blessing, knowing that you were called to this, that you may inherit a blessing *(1 Peter 3:8-9)*. Now hope does not disappoint, because the love of God has been poured out in our hearts by the Holy Spirit who was given to us *(Romans 5:5)*. Let love be without hypocrisy. Abhor what is evil. Cling to what is good *(Romans 12:9)*. The fruit of the Spirit is love *(Galatians 5:22)*.

OUR GRACIOUS, GIVING GOD

The eyes of all look expectantly to You [God] and You give them their food in due season. You open Your hand and satisfy the desire of every living thing. The LORD is righteous in all His ways, gracious in all His works. The LORD is near to all who call upon Him, to all who call upon Him in truth (*Psalm 145:15–18*). You [God] are good and do good; teach me Your statutes (*Psalm 119:68*). He [God] is a rewarder of those who diligently seek Him (*Hebrews 11:6*). For your Father knows the things you have need of before you ask Him (*Matthew 6:8*). "Ask, and it will be given to you; seek, and you will find; knock, and it will be opened to you. For everyone who asks receives, and he who seeks finds, and to him who knocks it will be opened. Or what man is there among you, if his son asks for bread, will give him a stone? Or if he asks for a fish, will he give him a serpent? If you then, being evil, know how to give good gifts to your children, how much more will your Father who is in heaven give good things to those who ask Him" *(Matthew 7:7-11)!* Those who seek You, LORD, shall not lack any good thing (*Psalm 34:10*). For the LORD God is a sun and a shield; the LORD will give grace and glory; no good thing will You withhold from those who walk uprightly (*Psalm 84:11*). Now to Him who is able to do exceedingly abundantly above all that we ask or think, according to the power that works in us, to Him be glory in the church by Christ Jesus to all generations, forever and ever. Amen (*Ephesians 3:20–21*). But seek first the kingdom of God and His righteousness, and all these things [necessities] shall be added to you (*Matthew 6:33*). He who did not spare His own Son, but delivered Him up for us all, how shall He not with Him also freely give us all things (*Romans 8:32*)?

BLESSED BE GOD FOREVER

Oh, bless our God, you peoples! And make the voice of His praise be heard (*Psalm 66:8*). Blessed be the Lord who daily loads us with benefits (*Psalm 68:19*). I will bless the LORD at all times; His praise shall continually be in my mouth (*Psalm 34:1*). Blessed be God, who has not turned away my prayer, nor His mercy from me! (*Psalm 66:20*). Daniel answered and said: "Blessed be the name of God forever and ever, for wisdom and might are His" (*Daniel 2:20*). I blessed the Most High and praised and honored Him who lives forever (*Daniel 4:34*). The LORD lives! Blessed be my rock! Let the God of my salvation be exalted (*Psalm 18:46*). "Blessed is the Lord God of Israel, for He has visited and redeemed His people" (*Luke 1:68*). "Blessed be Your glorious name, which is above all blessing and praise!" (*Nehemiah 9:5*). Blessed be the LORD, because He heard the voice of my supplications! (*Psalm 28:6*). Blessed be the God and Father of our Lord Jesus Christ, the Father of mercies and God of all comfort (*1 Corinthians 1:3*). "Bless the LORD, O my soul! O LORD my God, You are very great: You are clothed with honor and majesty" (*Psalm 104:1*). Bless the LORD, all His works, in all places of His dominion. Bless the LORD, O my soul! (*Psalm 103:22*). Blessed be His glorious name forever! And let the whole earth be filled with His glory. Amen and amen (*Psalm 72:19*). We will bless the LORD from this time forth and forevermore (*Psalm 115:18*). Sing to the LORD, bless His name; proclaim the good news of His salvation from day to day. Declare His glory among the nations, His wonders among all peoples. For great is the LORD and greatly to be praised (*Psalm 96:2–4*). Bless the LORD, O my soul; and all that is within me, bless His holy name! Bless the LORD, O my soul, and forget not all His benefits (*Psalm 103:1–2*).

ASSURED, STRENGTHENED, HELPED, AND UPHELD

But you, Israel, are my servant, Jacob whom I have chosen, the descendants of Abraham my friend. You whom I have taken from the ends of the earth, and called from its farthest regions, and said to you, "You are My servant, I have chosen you and have not cast you away; fear not for I am with you; be not dismayed, for I am Your God, I will strengthen you, yes, I will help you, I will uphold you with My righteous right hand" *(Isaiah 41:8–10)*. For Christ is the end of the law for righteousness to everyone who believes *(Romans 10:4)*. Of Him [God] you are in Christ Jesus, who became for us…righteousness *(1 Corinthians 1:30)*. The work of righteousness will be peace, and the effect of righteousness quietness and assurance forever *(Isaiah 32:17)*. He who believes in Him [Jesus] is not condemned *(John 3:18)*. "Because He [God] has appointed a day on which he will judge the world in righteousness by the man [Jesus] whom He has ordained. He has given assurance of this to all by raising Him from the dead" *(Acts 17:31)* that their hearts may be encouraged, being knit together in love, and attaining to all the riches of full assurance of understanding, to the knowledge of the mystery of God, both of the Father and of Christ *(Colossians 2:2)*; but grow in the grace and knowledge of our Lord and Savior Jesus Christ. To Him be the glory both now and forever. Amen *(2 Peter 3:18)*. God, who in various times and in various ways spoke in time past to the fathers by the prophets, has in these last days spoken to us by His Son, whom He has appointed heir of all things, through whom also He made the worlds; who being the brightness of His glory and the express image of His person, and upholds all things by the word of his power, when He had by Himself purged our sins, sat down at the right hand of the Majesty on high (*Hebrews 1:1–3*). For God did not appoint us to wrath, but to obtain salvation through our Lord Jesus Christ *(1 Thessalonians 5:9)*. Be of good courage, and He shall strengthen your heart, all you who hope in the LORD (*Psalm 31:24*).

SEALED BY THE SPIRIT TO WALK IN THE SPIRIT

"If you love Me [Jesus], keep My commandments (to believe in Jesus and to love God and others). And I will pray the Father, and He will give you another Helper [the Holy Spirit], that He may abide with you forever—the Spirit of truth" *(John 14:15–17)*. The helper, the Holy Spirit, whom the Father will send in My name, He will teach you all things, and bring to your remembrance all things that I have said *(John 14:26)*. In Him [Jesus] you also trusted, after you heard the word of truth, the gospel of your salvation; in whom also, having believed, you were sealed with the Holy Spirit of promise *(Ephesians 1:13)*. The Spirit, whom those believing in Him [Jesus] would receive *(John 7:39)*. You will receive power when the Holy Spirit has come upon you *(Acts 1:8)*. Truly I am full of power by the Spirit of the LORD *(Micah 3:8)*. Then the enemy comes in like a flood, the Spirit of the LORD will lift up a standard against him *(Isaiah 59:19)*. "Not by might nor by power, but by My Spirit," says the LORD of hosts *(Zechariah 4:6)*. But now we have been delivered from the law, having died to what we were held by, so that we should serve in the newness of the Spirit and not in the oldness of the letter *(Romans 7:6)*. There is therefore no condemnation to those who are in Christ Jesus, who do not walk according to the flesh, but according to the Spirit. For the law of the Spirit of life in Christ Jesus has made me free from the law of sin and death *(Romans 8:1–2)*. It is the Spirit who gives life; the flesh profits nothing. The words that I speak to you are spirit and they are life *(John 6:63)*. Now the Lord is the Spirit; and where the Spirit of the Lord is, there is liberty *(2 Corinthians 3:17)*. I say then: Walk in the Spirit, and you shall not fulfill the lust of the flesh. But if you are led by the Spirit, you are not under the law. If we live in the Spirit, let us also walk in the Spirit (*Galatians 5:16–25*). The Father of our Lord Jesus Christ,…that He would grant you…to be strengthened with might through His Spirit in the inner man, that Christ may dwell in your hearts through faith; that you, being rooted and ground in love…to know the love of Christ which passes knowledge; that you may be filled with all the fullness of God (*Ephesians 3:16–17, 19*). Now may the God of hope fill you with all joy and peace in believing, that you may abound in hope by the power of the Holy Spirit (*Romans 15:13*). Now hope does not disappoint, because the love of God has been pored out in our hearts by the Holy Spirit who was given to us *(Romans 5:5)*. The grace of the Lord Jesus Christ, and the love of God, and the communion of the Holy Spirit be with you all. Amen *(2 Corinthians 13:14)*.

MAKE ME FAITHFUL-HEARTED ME

Now set your heart and your soul to seek the LORD your God (*1 Chronicles 22:19*). You will seek the LORD your God, and you will find Him if you seek Him with all your heart and with all your soul (*Deuteronomy 4:29*); for man looks at the outward appearance, but the LORD looks at the heart (*1 Samuel 16:7*). For the eyes of the LORD run to and fro throughout the whole earth, to show Himself strong on behalf of those whose heart is loyal to Him (*2 Chronicles 16:9*). Oh, love the LORD, all you His saints! For the LORD preserves the faithful (*Psalm 31:23*). I [God] will betroth you to Me forever; yes, I will betroth you to Me in righteousness and mercy; I will betroth you to Me in loving-kindness and mercy; I will betroth you to Me in faithfulness, and you shall know the LORD (*Hosea 2:19–20*). But in a great house there are not only vessels of gold and silver, but also of wood and clay, some for honor and some for dishonor. Therefore if anyone cleanses himself from the latter, he will be a vessel for honor, sanctified [consecrated or set a side] and useful for the Master, prepared for every good work (*2 Timothy 2:20–21*). He who is faithful in what is least is faithful also in much; and he who is unjust in what is least is also unjust in much (*Luke 16:10*). Beloved, you do faithfully whatever you do for the brethren and for strangers (*3 John 1:5*). Abstain from every form of evil. Now may the God of peace Himself sanctify you completely; and may your whole spirit, soul, and body be preserved blameless at the coming of our Lord Jesus Christ. He who calls you is faithful, who also will do it (*1 Thessalonians 5:22-24*).

THE LORD, STRONG AND MIGHTY

"For the LORD your God dried up the waters of the Jordon before you [the children of Israel] until you had crossed over,… that all peoples of the earth may know the hand of the LORD, that it is mighty, that you may fear the LORD your God forever" (*Joshua 4:23–24*). For the eyes of the LORD run to and fro throughout the whole earth, to show Himself strong on behalf of those whose heart is loyal to Him (*2 Chronicles 16:9*). Who is the King of glory? The LORD strong and mighty, the Lord mighty in battle (*Psalm 24:8*). I will say to You Lord, "How awesome are Your works! Through the greatness of Your power Your enemies shall submit themselves to You" (*Psalm 66:3*). The LORD on high is mightier than the noise of many waters, than the mighty waves of the sea (*Psalm 93:4*). And to God belong the escapes from death (*Psalm 68:20*). God has spoken once, twice I have heard this: That power belongs to God (*Psalm 62:11*). "Blessed are You, LORD God of Israel, our Father, forever and ever. Yours O LORD, is the greatness, the power and the glory, the victory and the majesty; for all that is in heaven and in earth is Yours; Yours is the kingdom, O LORD, and You are exalted as head over all. Both riches and honor come from You, and You rein over all. In Your hand is power and might; in Your hand it is to make great and to give strength to all" (*1 Chronicles 29:10–12*). He who is in you is greater than he who is in the world (*1 John 4:4*). All the angels stood around the throne and the elders and the four living creatures, and fell on their faces before the throne and worshipped God, saying: "Amen! Blessing and glory and wisdom, thanksgiving and honor and power and might be to our God forever and ever. Amen" (*Revelation 7:11–12*).

SETTLING OUR SOULS

In righteousness you shall be established (*Isaiah 54:14*). The work of righteousness will be peace, and the effect of righteousness, quietness and assurance forever (*Isaiah 32:17*). My people will dwell in a peaceful habitation, in secure dwellings, and in quiet resting-places (*Isaiah 32:118*). For the gentiles will seek Him, and his resting-place shall be glorious (*Isaiah 11:10*). Rest in the LORD, and wait patiently for Him; cease from anger, and forsake wrath; do not fret it only causes harm (*Psalm 37:7*). Be still, and know that I am God (*Psalm 46:10*). Return to your rest, O my soul, for the LORD has dealt bountifully with you (*Psalm 116:7*). Surely I have calmed and quieted my soul, like a weaned child with his mother; like a weaned child shall my soul be within me. O Israel hope in the LORD from this time forth and forever (*Psalm 131:2–3*). "Take My [Jesus] yoke upon you and learn from Me, for I am gentle and lowly in heart, and you will find rest for your souls. For My yoke is easy and My burden is light" (*Matthew 11:29–30*). But may the God of all grace, who called us to His eternal glory by Christ Jesus, after you have suffered a while, perfect, establish, strengthen, and settle you. To Him be the glory and the dominion forever and ever. Amen (*1 Peter 5:10–11*).

MIGHTY MEANINGFUL TO BE MERCIFUL!

The merciful man does good to own soul, but he who is cruel troubles his own flesh (*Proverbs 11:17*). But love your enemies, do good, and lend, hoping for nothing in return; and your reward will be great, and you will be sons of the Most High. For He is kind to the unthankful and evil. Therefore be merciful, just as your Father also is merciful (*Luke 6:35–36*). What is desired in a man is kindness (*Proverbs 19:22*). The discretion of a man makes him slow to anger, and his glory is to overlook a transgression (*Proverbs 19:11*). And forgive us our debts, as we forgive our debtors. For if you forgive men their trespasses your Heavenly Father will also forgive you. But if you do not forgive men their trespasses, neither will your Father forgive your trespasses (*Matthew 6:12, 14–15*). Whenever you stand praying, if you have anything against anyone, forgive him, that your Father in heaven may also forgive you your trespasses. But if you do not forgive, neither will your Father in heaven forgive your trespasses (*Mark 11:25–26*). And be kind to one another, tenderhearted, forgiving one another, even as God in Christ forgave you (*Ephesians 4:32*). So speak and so do as those who will be judged by the law of liberty. For judgment is without mercy to the one who has shown no mercy. Mercy triumphs over judgment (*James 2:12–13*). Blessed are the merciful, for they shall obtain mercy (*Matthew 5:7*).

FINDING FREEDOM

What shall we say then? Shall we continue in sin that grace may abound? Certainly not! How shall we who died to sin live any longer in it? (*Romans 6:1–2*). If we confess our sins, He [God] is faithful and just to forgive us our sins and to cleanse us from all unrighteousness (*1 John 1:9*). These things I write to you, so that you may not sin. And if anyone sins, we have an advocate with the Father, Jesus Christ the righteous. And He Himself [Jesus] is the propitiation [the one who makes appeasement] for our sins (*1 John 2:1–2*). But if we walk in the light as He is in the light, we have fellowship with one another, and the blood of Jesus Christ His [God's] Son cleanses us from all sin (*1 John 1:7*). Likewise you also reckon yourselves to be dead to sin, but alive to God in Christ Jesus our Lord (*Romans 6:11*). Brethren, we are debtors—not to the flesh, to live according to the flesh (*Romans 8:12*). And having been set free from sin, you became slaves of righteousness (*Romans 6:18*). And do not present your members as instruments of unrighteousness to sin, but present yourselves to God as being alive from the dead, and your members as instruments of righteousness to God. For sin shall not have dominion over you, for you are not under law but under grace (*Romans 6:13–14*). I [Paul the apostle] say then: Walk in the Spirit, and you shall not fulfill the lust of the flesh. *Galatians 5:16* Whoever abides in Him [Jesus] does not sin (*1 John 3:6*). "Most assuredly, I [the Lord Jesus Christ] say to you, whoever commits sin is a slave to sin. And a slave does not abide in the house forever, but a son abides forever. Therefore if the Son makes you free, you shall be free indeed (*John 8:34–36*). For you are all sons of God through faith in Christ Jesus (*Galatians 3:26*). Who shall bring a charge against God's elect? It is God who justifies. Who is he who condemns? It is Christ who died, and furthermore is also risen, who is even at the right hand of God, who also makes intercession for us (*Romans 8:33–34*). Therefore if anyone is in Christ, he is a new creation; old things have passed away; behold all things have become new (*2 Corinthians 5:17*). Now the Lord is the Spirit; and where the Spirit of the Lord is, there is liberty (*2 Corinthians 3:17*). Stand fast therefore in the liberty by which Christ has made us free, and do not be entangled again with the yoke of bondage [looking to circumcision or anything other than faith in Christ] (*Galatians 5:1*). The sting of death is sin, and the strength of sin is the law. But thanks be to God, who gives us the victory through our Lord Jesus Christ *(1 Corinthians 15:56-57).*

WAITING IN YOUR WINGS

How often I have wanted to gather your children together, as a hen gathers her chicks under her wings, but you were not willing! (*Matthew 23:37*). He shall cover You with His feathers, and under His wings you shall take refuge; His truth shall be your shield and buckler [hand-held shield]. You shall not be afraid of the terror by night, nor of the arrow that flies by day, nor of the pestilence that walks in darkness, nor of the destruction that lays waste at noonday (*Psalm 91:4–6*). How precious is Your loving-kindness O God! Therefore the children of men put their trust under the shadow of Your wings (*Psalm 36:7*). For you have been a shelter for me, a strong tower from the enemy. I will abide in Your tabernacle forever; I will trust in the shelter of Your wings (*Psalm 61:3–4*). Be merciful to me, O God, be merciful to me! For my soul trusts in You; and in the shadow of Your wings I will make my refuge, until these calamities have passed by (*Psalm 57:1*). Because You have been my help, therefore in the shadow of Your wings I will rejoice (*Psalm 63:7*). Keep me as the apple of Your eye; hide me under the shadow of Your wings (*Psalm 17:8*).

OUR OWN WICKEDNESS WILL CORRECT US

My people would not heed My voice, and Israel would have none of Me. So I gave them over to their own stubborn heart, to walk in their own counsels (*Psalm 81:11–12*). The backslider in heart will be filled with his own ways, but a good man will be satisfied from above (*Proverbs 14:14*). Your own wickedness will also correct you, and your backsliding will rebuke you (*Jeremiah 2:19*). "For Israel is stubborn like a stubborn calf; now the LORD will let them forage [search on their own] like a lamb in open country (*Hosea 4:16*). I will instruct you and teach you in the way you should go; I will guide you with my eye. Do not be like a horse or the mule, which have no understanding, which must be harnessed with bit and bridle, else they will not come near you (*Psalm 32:9*). He who keeps instruction is in the way of life, but he who refuses correction goes astray (*Proverbs 10:17*). He who disdains instruction despises his own soul, but he who heeds rebuke gets understanding (*Proverbs 15:32*). Apply your heart to instruction, and your ears to words of knowledge (*Proverbs 23:12*). All scripture is given by inspiration of God, and is profitable for doctrine, for reproof, for correction, for instruction in righteousness (*2 Timothy 3:16*). Listen to counsel and receive instruction, that you may be wise in your latter days (*Proverbs 19:20*).

TRUSTING AND TRIUMPHING THROUGH TRIBULATION

For to you it has been granted on behalf of Christ, not only to believe in Him, but also to suffer for His sake (*Philippians 1:29*). "In the world you will have tribulation; but be of good cheer, I have overcome the world" (*John 16:33*). Strengthening the souls of the disciples, exhorting them to continue in the faith, and saying, "We must through many tribulations enter the kingdom of God" (*Acts 14:22*). To establish you and encourage you concerning your faith, that no one should be shaken by these afflictions; for you yourselves know that we are appointed to this. For, in fact, we told you before, when we were with you that we would suffer tribulation, just as it happened, and you know (*1 Thessalonians 3:4*). Yes, and all who desire to live Godly in Christ Jesus will suffer persecution (*2 Timothy 3:12*). Beloved, do not think it strange concerning the fiery trial which is to try you, as though some strange thing happened to you; but rejoice to the extent that you partake of Christ's sufferings, that when His glory is revealed, you may also be glad with exceeding joy (*1 Peter 4:12–13*); not lagging in diligence, fervent in spirit, serving the Lord; rejoicing in hope, patient in tribulation, continuing steadfast in prayer (*Romans 12:11–12*). No temptation has overtaken you except such as is common to man; but God is faithful, you will not allow you to be tempted beyond what you are able, but with the temptation will also make the way of escape, that you may be able to bear it (*1 Corinthians 10:13*). For in that He [Jesus Christ] Himself has suffered, being tempted, He is able to aid those who are tempted (*Hebrews 2:18*). We have such trust through Christ toward God. Not that we are sufficient of ourselves to think of anything as being from ourselves, but our sufficiency is from God (*2 Corinthians 3:4–5*). Who [the Father of our Lord Jesus Christ] comforts us in all our tribulation, that we may be able to comfort those who are in any trouble, with the comfort with which we ourselves are comforted by God (*1 Corinthians 1:4*). And not only that, but we also glory in tribulations, knowing that tribulation produces perseverance; and perseverance, character; and character, hope (*Romans 5:3*) that the genuineness of your faith, being much more precious than gold that perishes, though it is tested by fire, may be found to praise, honor, and glory at the revelation of Jesus Christ (*1 Peter 1:7*).

GUARDING GOODNESS

Repay no one evil for evil, but have regard for good things in the sight of all men. If it is possible as much as depends on you, live peaceably with all men. Beloved do not avenge yourselves, but rather give place to wrath; for it is written, "Vengeance is Mine, I will repay," says the Lord (*Romans 12:17–20*). He who does wrong will be repaid for what he has done, and there is no partiality (*Colossians 3:25*), but rejoice to the extent that you partake of Christ's sufferings, that when His glory is revealed, you may also be glad with exceeding joy. If you are reproached for the name of Christ, blessed are you, for the Spirit of glory and of God rests upon you. On their part He is blasphemed, but on your part He is glorified (*1 Peter 4:13–14*). Yet if anyone suffers as a Christian, let him not be ashamed, but let him glorify God in this matter (*1 Peter 4:16*). Do not be overcome by evil, but overcome evil with good (*Romans 12:21*). Therefore let those who suffer according to the will of God commit their souls to Him in doing good, as to a faithful Creator (*1 Peter 4:19*).

THE BEST IS YET TO COME

And truly if they had called to mind that country from which they had come out, they would have had opportunity to return. But now they desire a better, that is, a heavenly country. Therefore God is not ashamed to be called their God, for He has prepared a city for them (*Hebrews 11:15–16*), looking for the blessed hope and glorious appearing of our great God and Savior Jesus Christ (*Titus 2:13*). Jesus Christ who has gone into heaven and is at the right hand of God, angels and authorities and powers having been made subject to Him (*1 Peter 3:21–22*). Set your mind on things above, not on things on the earth. For you died and your life is hidden with Christ in God. When Christ who is your life appears, then you also will appear with Him in glory (*Colossians 3:3–4*). We, according to His promise, look for new heavens and a new earth in which righteousness [rightness and justice] dwell (*2 Peter 3:13*). But I do not want you to be ignorant, brethren, concerning those who have fallen asleep [died] lest you sorrow as others who have no hope. For if we believe that Jesus died and rose again, even so God will bring with Him those who sleep in Jesus. For this we say by the word of the Lord, that we who remain alive and remain until the coming of the Lord will by no means precede those who are asleep. For the Lord Himself will descend from heaven with a shout, with the voice of an archangel, and with the trumpet of God. And the dead in Christ will rise first. Then we who are alive and remain shall be caught up together with them in the air. And thus we shall always be with the Lord. Therefore comfort one another with these words (*1 Thessalonians 4:13–18*). But as it is written: "Eye has not seen, nor ear heard, nor have entered into the heart of man the things which God has prepared for those who love Him" (*1 Corinthians 2:9*). For we know that if our earthly house, this tent, is destroyed, we have a building from God, a house not made with hands, eternal in the heavens *(2 Corinthians 5:1)*.

IF YOU WOULD BE ROYALTY, TREAT PEOPLE ROYALLY

Beloved, if God so loved us [by sending His Son to die for our sins], we also ought to love one another (*1 John 4:11*). He has shown you, O man, what is good; and what does the LORD require of you but to do justly, to love mercy, and walk humbly with your God? (*Micah 6:8*). Whoever desires to be great among you shall be your servant. And whoever of you desires to be first shall be slave of all (*Mark 10:43–44*). If you really fulfill the royal law according to the Scripture, "You shall love your neighbor as yourself," you do well (*James 2:8*). Therefore, whatever you want men to do to you, do also to them, for this is the Law and the Prophets (*Matthew 7:12*). And this I pray, that your love may abound still more and more in knowledge and all discernment, that you may approve the things that are excellent, that you may be sincere and without offence till the day of Christ, being filled with the fruits of righteousness which are by Christ Jesus, to the glory and praise of God (*Philippians 1:9–11*). For this is the will of God, that by doing good you may put to silence the ignorance of foolish men -- as free, yet not using liberty as a cloak for vise [bad behavior], but as bondservants of God. Honor all people. Love the brotherhood. Fear God. Honor the king *(1 Peter 2:15-17)*.

NOT FACING TEMPTATION ALONE

No temptation has overtaken you except such as is common to man; but God is faithful, who will not allow you to be tempted beyond what you are able, but with the temptation will also make the way of escape, that you may be able to bear it (*1 Corinthians 10:13*). Blessed is the man who endures temptation, for when he has been approved, he will receive the crown of life, which the Lord has promised to those who love Him. *Romans 1:12* The Lord knows how to deliver the godly out of temptations (*2 Peter 2:9*). For in that He [Jesus] Himself has suffered, being tempted, He is able to aid those who are tempted (*Hebrews 2:18*). Seeing then that we have a great High Priest [Jesus] who has passed through the heavens, Jesus the Son of God, let us hold fast our confession. For we do not have a High Priest who cannot sympathize with our weaknesses, but was in all points tempted as we are, yet without sin. Let us therefore come boldly to the throne of grace, that we may obtain mercy and find grace to help in time of need (*Hebrews 4:14–16*). He will again have compassion on us, and will subdue our iniquities. You will cast all our sins into the depths of the sea *(Micah 7:19)*.

LETTING THE WORD DO ITS WORK

Therefore, laying aside all malice, all deceit, hypocrisy, envy, and all evil speaking, as new born babes, desire the pure milk of the word, that you may grow thereby, if indeed you have tasted that the Lord is gracious *(1 Peter 2:1–3)*. Let the word of Christ dwell in you richly in all wisdom, teaching and admonishing one another in psalms and hymns and spiritual songs, singing with grace in your hearts to the Lord *(Colossians 3:16)*. Take heed to yourself and to the doctrine. Continue in them, for in doing this you will save both yourself and those who hear you *(1 Timothy 4:16)*. So now, brethren, I commend you to God, and to the word of His grace, which is able to build you up and give you an inheritance among all who are sanctified *(Acts 20:32)*. Therefore lay aside all filthiness and overflow of wickedness, and receive with meekness the implanted word, which is able to save your souls *(James 1:21)*. The Holy Scriptures, which are able to make you wise for salvation through faith which is in Christ Jesus. All Scripture is given by inspiration of God, and is profitable for doctrine, for reproof, for correction, for instruction in righteousness, that the man of God may be complete, thoroughly equipped for every good work *(2 Timothy 3:15-17)*. You must continue in the things which you have learned and been assured of *(2 Timothy 3:14)*.

HOW CHIC TO BE MEEK

Now Moses was very humble [meek: mild of temper, gentle, not easily provoked, given to forbearance under injuries, submissive to the Divine will, uncomplaining, not proud], more than all men who were on the face of the earth (*Numbers 12:3*). "Take My [Jesus] yoke upon you and learn from me, for I am gentle [meek] and lowly in heart, and you will find rest for your souls" (*Matthew 11:29*). Seek the LORD all you meek of the earth, who have upheld His justice. Seek righteousness, seek humility. It may be that you will be hidden in the day of the LORD's anger (*Zephaniah 2:3*). But with righteousness He shall judge the poor, and with equity [fairness and impartiality] for the meek of the earth (*Isaiah 11:4*), and the humble [meek] He teaches His way (*Psalm 25:9*). The LORD lifts up the humble [meek] (*Psalm 147:6*). The meek shall inherit the earth, and shall delight themselves in the abundance of peace (*Psalm 37:11*). The humble [meek] also shall increase their joy in the LORD, and the poor among men shall rejoice in the Holy One of Israel (*Isaiah 29:19*). "Blessed are the meek, for they shall inherit the earth" (*Matthew 5:5*). A servant of the Lord must not quarrel but be gentle to all, able to teach, patient, in humility [meekness] correcting those who are in opposition (*2 Timothy 2:24–25*). Therefore, as the elect of God, holy and beloved, put on tender mercies, kindness, humility, meekness, longsuffering (*Colossians 3:12*). Do not let your adornment be merely outward... Rather let it be the hidden person of the heart, with the incorruptible beauty of a gentle [meek] and quiet spirit, which is precious in the sight of God (*1 Peter 3:3–4*). To speak evil of no one, to be peaceable, gentle, showing humility [meekness] to all men (*Titus 3:2*). For the LORD takes pleasure in His people; He will beautify the humble [meek] with salvation (*Psalm 149:4*). Put on the Lord Jesus Christ, and make no provision for the flesh, to fulfill its lusts *(Romans 13:14)*.

SAVED FROM SHAME

I cling to your testimonies; O LORD, do not put me to shame! (*Psalm 119:31*). When pride comes, then comes shame (*Proverbs 11:2*). For He shall stand at the right hand of the poor, to save him from those who condemn him (*Psalm 109:31*). The wicked watches the righteous, and seeks to slay him. The LORD will not leave him in his hand, nor condemn him when he is judged (*Psalm 37:32–33*). Keep my soul, and deliver me; let me not be ashamed, for I put my trust in You. Let integrity and uprightness preserve me, for I wait for you (*Psalm 25:20–21*). Make Your face shine upon Your servant; save me for Your mercy's sake. Do not let me be ashamed, O LORD, for I have called upon You (*Psalm 31:16–17*). O my God, I trust in You; let me not be ashamed; let not my enemies triumph over me. Indeed, let no one who waits on You be ashamed (*Psalm 25:2–3*). "I am the LORD, for they shall not be ashamed who wait for Me" (*Isaiah 49:23*). "Behold, I [God] lay in Zion a chief cornerstone, elect, precious, and he who believes in Him [Jesus] will by no means be put to shame [permanent shame]" (*1 Peter 2:6*). "I counsel you to buy from Me [Jesus] gold refined in fire, that you may be rich; and white garments, that you may be clothed, that the shame of your nakedness may not be revealed; and anoint your eyes with eye salve, that you may see" (*Revelation 3:18*). "Behold, I am coming as a thief. Blessed is he who watches, and keeps his garments, lest he walk in naked and they see his shame" (*Revelation 16:15*). So they [the disciples] departed from the presents of the council, rejoicing that they were counted worthy to suffer shame for His [Jesus] name (*Acts 45:41*). Behold at that time I will deal with all who afflict you; I will save the lame, and gather those who were driven out; I will appoint them for praise and fame in every land where they were put to shame (*Zephaniah 3:19*). Blessed are those persecuted for righteousness' sake, for theirs is the kingdom of heaven. "Blessed are you when they revile and persecute you, and say all kinds of evil against you falsely for My sake. Rejoice and be exceedingly glad, for great is your reward in heaven, for so they persecuted the prophets who were before you (*Matthew 5:10–12*).

HIS UPHOLDING RIGHT HAND

Indeed My hand has laid the foundation of the earth, and My right hand has stretched out the heavens (*Isaiah 48:13*). Your right hand, O LORD, has become glorious in power (*Exodus 15:6*). O LORD GOD, You have begun to show Your servant Your greatness and Your mighty hand, for what god is there in heaven or on earth who can do anything like Your works and Your mighty deeds? (*Deuteronomy 3:24*). Both riches and honor come from You, and You rein over all. In Your right hand is power and might; in Your right hand it is to make great and to give strength to all (*1 Chronicles 29:12*). For they did not gain possession of the land by their own sword, nor did their own arm save them; but it was Your right hand, Your arm, and the light of Your countenance, because You favored them (*Psalm 44:3*). Though I walk in the midst of trouble, You will revive me; You will stretch out Your hand against the wrath of my enemies, and Your right hand will save me (*Psalm 138:7*). Oh, sing to the LORD a new song! For He has done marvelous things; His right hand and His holy arm have gained Him the victory (*Psalm 98:1*). The voice of rejoicing and salvation is in the tents of the righteous; the right hand of the LORD does valiantly. The right hand of the LORD is exalted; the right hand of the LORD does valiantly (*Psalm 118:15–16*). What You give them they gather in; You open Your hand, and they are filled with good (*Psalm 104:28*). Let Your hand become my help, for I have chosen Your precepts [to obey His counsel] (*Psalm 119:173*). You have given me the shield of Your salvation; Your right hand has held me up (*Psalm 18:35*). So I was encouraged, as the hand of the LORD my God was upon me (*Ezra 7:28*). "There is no one who can deliver out of My hand; I work, and who will reverse it?" (*Isaiah 43:13*). You are my strength. Into Your hand

I commit my spirit; You have redeemed me, O LORD God of truth (*Psalm 31:4–5*). Show Your marvelous lovingkindness by Your right hand, O You who save those who trust in You from those who rise up against them *(Psalm 17:7)*. You will show me the path of life; in Your presence is fullness of joy; at Your right hand are pleasures forevermore (*Psalm 16:11*).

HEAVEN, OUR HOME

"Do not lay up for yourselves treasures on earth, where rust and moth destroy and where thieves break in and steal; but lay up for yourselves treasures in heaven, where neither moth nor rust destroys and where thieves do not break in and steal. For where your treasure is, there your heart will be also" (*Matthew 6:19–21*). Christ was offered once to bear the sins of many. To those who eagerly wait for Him He will appear a second time, apart from sin, for salvation (*Hebrews 9:28*). For our citizenship is in heaven, from which we also eagerly wait for the Savior, the Lord Jesus Christ (*Philippians 3:20*). If then you were raised with Christ, seek those things, which are above, where Christ is sitting at the right hand of God. Set your mind on things above, not on things on the earth. For you died, and your life is hidden with Christ in God. When Christ who is our life appears, then you also will appear with Him in glory (*Colossians 3:1–4*) to an inheritance incorruptible and undefiled and that does not fade away, reserved in heaven for you who are kept by the power of God through faith for salvation ready to be revealed in the last time (*1 Peter 1:4–5*),…knowing that you have a better and an enduring possession for yourselves in heaven. Therefore do not cast away your confidence, which has great reward (*Hebrews 10:34–35*), while we do not look at the things which are seen, but at the things which are not seen. For the things which are seen are temporary, but the things which are not seen are eternal (*2 Corinthians 4:18*). Looking unto Jesus, the author and finisher of our faith, who for the joy the joy that was set before Him endured the cross, despising the shame, and has sat down at the right hand of the throne of God (*Hebrews 12:2*). For we know that if our earthly house, this tent, is destroyed, we have a building from God, a house not made with hands, eternal in the heavens (*2 Corinthians 5:1*). And thus we shall always be with the Lord (*1 Thessalonians 4:17*).

A FUTURE AND A HOPE

"For My thoughts are not your thoughts, nor are your ways My ways," says the LORD. For as the heavens are higher than the earth, so are My ways higher than your ways, and My thoughts than your thoughts *(Isaiah 55:8–9)*. For I know the thoughts that I think toward you, says the LORD, thoughts of peace and not of evil, to give you a future and a hope *(Jeremiah 29:11)*. In Him [Jesus Christ] we have redemption through His blood, the forgiveness of sins, according to the riches of His grace *(Ephesians 1:7)*. What then shall we say to these things? If God is for us, who can be against us? He [God the Father] who did not spare His own Son, but delivered Him up for us all, how shall He not with Him also freely give us all things? *(Romans 8:31–32)*. We are not those who draw back to perdition, but those who believe to the saving of the soul *(Hebrews 10:39)*. Therefore do not cast away your confidence, which has great reward *(Hebrews 10:35)*. "Blessed is the man who trusts in the LORD, and whose hope is the LORD" *(Jeremiah 17:7)*. He [Jesus] indeed was foreordained before the foundation of the world, but was manifest in these last times for you who through Him believe in God, who raised Him from the dead and gave Him glory, so your faith and hope are in God *(1 Peter 1:20–21)*. And we know that all things work together for good to those who love God, to those who are the called according to His purpose *(Romans 8:28)*. Being confident of this very thing, that He who has begun a good work in you will complete it until the day of Jesus Christ *(Philippians 1:6)*. And thus we shall always be with the Lord *(1 Thessalonians 4:17)*.

PLANTED IN PERFECT PEACE

For "He who would love life and see good days, let him refrain his tongue from evil, and his lips from speaking deceit. Let him turn away from evil and do good; let him seek peace and pursue it. For the eyes of the LORD are on the righteous, and his ears are open to their prayers; but the face of the LORD is against those who do evil" (*1 Peter 3:10–12*). Now may the God of peace Himself sanctify you completely (*1 Thessalonians 5:23*). The LORD bless you and keep you; the LORD make His face shine upon you, and be gracious to you; the LORD lift up His countenance upon you, and give you peace (*Numbers 6:24–26*). To those who are called, sanctified by God the Father, and preserved in Jesus Christ: Mercy, peace, and love be multiplied to you, beloved (*Jude 1:1–3*). Among whom you also are the called of Jesus Christ, beloved of God, called to be saints. Grace to you and peace from God our Father and the Lord Jesus Christ (*Romans 1:6–7*). My people will dwell in a peaceful habitation, in secure dwellings, and in quiet resting places (*Isaiah 32:18*). I will both lie down in peace, and sleep; for You alone, O LORD, make me to dwell in safety (*Psalm 4:8*). For the mountains shall depart and the hills be removed, but My kindness shall not depart from you, nor shall My covenant of peace be removed," says the LORD who has mercy on you (*Isaiah 54:10*). "How beautiful upon the mountains are the feet of him who brings good news, who proclaims peace, who brings glad tidings of good things, who proclaims salvation who say to Zion, your God reins!" (*Isaiah 52:7*). Now may the Lord of peace Himself give you peace always in every way. The Lord be with you all
(*2 Thessalonians 3:16*). LORD, You will establish peace for us (*Isaiah 26:12*). The LORD will give strength to His people; the LORD will bless His people with peace (*Psalm 29:11*). "Peace I

[Christ] leave with you, My peace I give to you; not as the world gives do I give to you. Let not your heart be troubled, neither let it be afraid (*John 14:27*). You will keep him in perfect peace, whose mind is stayed on You, because he trusts in You. Trust in the LORD forever, for in Yah the LORD, is everlasting strength (*Isaiah 26:3–4*). Be anxious for nothing, but in everything by prayer and supplication, with thanksgiving, let your requests be made known to God; and the peace of God, which passes all understanding, will guard your hearts and minds through Christ Jesus (*Philippians 4:6–7*). Having been justified by faith, we have peace with God through our Lord Jesus Christ, through whom also we have access by faith into this grace in which we stand, and rejoice in hope of the glory of God *(Romans 5:1)*. Peace to all who are in Christ Jesus (*1 Peter 5:14*).

ENCOURAGED TO ADD AND PURSUE

As righteousness leads to life, so he who pursues evil pursues it to his own death (*Proverbs 11:19*). Nevertheless the solid foundation of God stands, having this seal: "Let everyone who names the name of Christ depart from iniquity" (*2 Timothy 2:19*). Beloved, now we are the children of God; and it has not yet been revealed what we shall be, but we know that when He is revealed, we shall be like Him, for we shall see Him as He is. And everyone who has this hope in him purifies himself, just as He is pure (*1 John 3:2–3*). As for me, I will see Your face in righteousness; I shall be satisfied when I awake in Your likeness (*Psalm 17:15*). But those who desire to be rich fall into temptation and a snare, and into many foolish and harmful lusts which drown men in destruction and perdition [unrepentant state]. For the love of money is a root of all kinds of evil, for which some have strayed from the faith in their greediness, and pierced themselves through with many sorrows. But you, O man of God, flee these things and pursue righteousness, godliness, faith, love, patience, gentleness. Fight the good fight of faith, lay hold on eternal life, to which you were called and have confessed the good confession in the presence of many witnesses (*1 Timothy 6:9–12*). Flee also youthful lusts; but pursue righteousness, faith, love, peace with those who call on the Lord out of a pure heart (*2 Timothy 2:22*). Blessed are those who hunger and thirst for righteousness, for they shall be filled (*Matthew 5:6*). Give all diligence, add to your faith virtue, to virtue knowledge, to knowledge self-control, to self-control perseverance, to perseverance godliness, to godliness brotherly kindness and to brotherly kindness love. For if these things are yours and abound, you will be neither barren nor unfruitful in the knowledge of our Lord Jesus Christ. For He who lacks these things is shortsighted, even to blindness, and has forgotten and has forgotten that he was cleansed from his old sins. Therefore brethren, be even more diligent to make your call and election sure, for if you do these things you will never stumble; for so an entrance will be supplied to you abundantly into the everlasting kingdom of our Lord and Savior Jesus Christ (*2 Peter 1:5–11*).

IT WORKS TO WAIT

Show me Your ways, O LORD; teach me Your paths. Lead me in Your truth and teach me, for You are the God of my salvation; on You I wait all the day (*Psalm 25:5*). The LORD is good to those who wait for Him. It is good that one should hope and wait quietly for the salvation of the LORD (*Lamentations 3:25–26*). Rest in the LORD, and wait patiently for Him (*Psalm 37:7*). For thus says the Lord GOD, the Holy One of Israel: "In returning and rest you shall be saved; in quietness and confidence shall be your strength" (*Isaiah 30:15*). I waited patiently for the LORD; and He inclined to me, and heard my cry. He also brought me up out of a horrible pit, out of the miry clay, and set my feet upon a rock, and established my steps (*Psalm 40:1–2*). Observe mercy and justice, and wait on your God continually (*Hosea 12:6*). Wait on the LORD; be of good courage, and He shall strengthen your heart; wait, I say, on the LORD! (*Psalm 27:14*). Wait on the LORD, and keep His way, and He shall exalt you to inherit the land (*Psalm 37:34*). Therefore I will look to the LORD; I will wait for the God of my salvation; my God will hear me (*Micah 7:7*). I wait for the LORD, my soul waits, and in His word I do hope. My soul waits for the LORD more than those who watch for the morning—yes, more than those who watch for the morning. O Israel, hope in the LORD; for with the LORD there is mercy, and with Him is abundant redemption. And He shall redeem Israel from all his iniquities (*Psalm 130:5–8*). My soul wait silently for God alone, for my expectation is from Him; He only is my rock and my salvation; He is my defense; I shall not be moved (*Psalm 62:5–6*). The LORD will wait, that He may be gracious to you; and therefore He will be exalted, that He may have mercy on you. For the LORD is a God of justice; blessed are all those who wait for Him (*Isaiah 30:18*). But those who wait on the LORD shall renew their strength; they shall mount up with wings like eagles, they shall run and not be weary, they shall walk and not faint (*Isaiah 40:31*). Do not say, "I will recompense evil"; wait for the LORD, and He shall save you (*Proverbs 20:22*). Indeed, let no one who waits on You be ashamed; let those be ashamed who deal treacherously without cause (*Psalm 25:3*). Keep my soul, and deliver me; let me not be ashamed, for I put my trust in You. Let integrity and uprightness preserve me, for I wait for You (*Psalm 25:20–22*). "For they shall not be ashamed who wait for me [God]" (*Isaiah 49:23*). For since the beginning of the world men have not heard nor perceived by ear, nor has eye seen any God besides You, who acts for the one who waits for Him (*Isaiah 64:4*).

MAKING YOUR HEART HIS

You shall love the LORD your God with all your heart, with all your soul, and with all your strength (*Deuteronomy 6:5*). Nevertheless I have this against you, that you have left your first love (*Revelation 2:4*). And He [Jesus] died for all, that those who live should live no longer for themselves, but for Him who died for them and rose again (*2 Corinthians 5:15*). If you love Me, keep My commandments (*John 14:15*). Jesus said to him, "You shall love the LORD your God with all your heart, with all your soul, and with all your mind." This is the first and greatest commandment. And the second is like it: "You shall love your neighbor as yourself." "On these two commandments hang all the law and the prophets" (*Matthew 22:37–40*). He who loves father or mother more than Me is not worthy of Me. And he who loves son or daughter more than Me is not worthy of Me (*Matthew 10:37*). Listen, O daughter, consider and incline your ear; forget your own people also, and your father's house; so the king will greatly desire your beauty (*Psalm 45:10–11*). Behold, I stand at the door and knock. If anyone hears My voice and opens the door, I will come in to him and dine with him and He with me (*Revelation 3:20*). The Spirit and the bride say, "Come!" and let him who thirsts come. Whoever desires, let him take the water of life freely (*Revelation 22:17*). Delight yourself also in the Lord, and He shall give you the desires of your heart (*Psalm 37:4*). "Eye has not seen, nor ear heard, nor have entered into the heart of man the things which God has prepared for those who love Him" (*1 Corinthians 2:9*). For the eyes of the LORD run to and fro throughout the whole earth, to show Himself strong on behalf of those whose heart is loyal to Him (*2 Chronicles 16:9*). Draw near to God and He will draw near to you (*James 4:8*).

ESTABLISHED ETERNALLY

But God demonstrates His love toward us, in that while we were still sinners, Christ died for us. Much more then, having now been justified by His blood, we shall be saved from wrath through Him. For if when we were enemies we were reconciled to God through the death of His Son, much more, having been reconciled, we shall be saved by His life (*Romans 5:8–10*). But God be thanked that though you were slaves to sin, yet you obeyed from the heart that form of doctrine to which you were delivered. And being set free from sin, you became a slave to righteousness (*Romans 6:17–18*). To them [us] God willed to make known what are the riches of this mystery among the gentiles: which is Christ in you the hope of glory (*Colossians 1:27*). We are bound to give thanks to God always for you, brethren beloved of the Lord, because God from the beginning chose you for salvation through sanctification by the Spirit and belief in the truth, to which He called you by our gospel, for the obtaining of the glory of our Lord Jesus Christ. Therefore, brethren, stand fast and hold the traditions which you were taught, whether by word or our epistle. Now may our Lord Jesus Christ Himself, and our God and Father, who loved us and given us everlasting consolation and good hope by grace, comfort your hearts and establish you in every good word and work (*2 Thessalonians 2:13–17*). The Lord is faithful, who will establish you and guard you from the evil one (*2 Thessalonians 3:3*). But may the God of all grace, who called us to His eternal glory by Christ Jesus, after you have suffered a while, perfect, establish, strengthen and settle you. To Him be the glory and dominion forever and ever. Amen (*1 Peter 5:10–11*). And may the Lord make you increase and abound in love to one another and to all, just as we [the Apostle Paul and his fellow workers] do to you, so He may establish your hearts blameless in holiness before our God and Father at the coming of our Lord Jesus Christ with all His saints (*1 Thessalonians 3:12–13*).

AFFLICTED TO BE LIBERATED

For Israel is stubborn like a stubborn calf; now the LORD will let them forage like a lamb in open country (*Hosea 4:16*). "I will return to My place till they acknowledge their offense. Then they will seek My face; in their affliction they will earnestly seek Me" *(Hosea 5:15)*. It is good for me that I have been afflicted, that I may learn Your statutes (*Psalm 119:71*). For our light affliction, which is but for a moment, is working for us a far more exceeding and eternal weight of glory (*2 Corinthians 4:17*),... though now for a little while, if need be, you have been grieved by various trials, that the genuineness of your faith, being much more precious than gold which perishes, though it be tested with fire, may be found to praise, honor, and glory at the revelation of Jesus Christ (*1 Peter 1:6–7*). And our hope for you is steadfast, because we know that as you are partakers of the sufferings, so also you will partake in the consolation (*2 Corinthians 1:7*). Jesus answered them, "Most assuredly I say to you, whoever commits sin is a slave to sin. And a slave does not abide in the house forever, but a son abides forever. Therefore if the Son makes you free, you shall be free indeed" (*John 8:34–36*). For you, brethren, have been called to liberty; only do not use liberty as an opportunity for the flesh, but through love serve one another. For all the law is fulfilled in one word, even in this: "You shall love your neighbor as yourself." But if you bite and devour one another, beware lest you be consumed by one another! (*Galatians 5:13–15*). Many are the afflictions of the righteous, but the LORD delivers him out of them all (*Psalm 34:19*). Now to Him who is able to keep you from stumbling, and to present you faultless before the presence of His glory with exceeding joy, to God our Savior, who alone is wise, be glory and majesty, dominion and power, both now and forever. Amen (*Jude 1:24–25*). Sing, O heavens! Be joyful, O earth! And break out in singing, O mountains! For the LORD has comforted His people, and will have mercy on His afflicted. (*Isaiah 49:13*).

A LITTLE IS A LOT WITH THE LORD

He who is greedy for gain troubles his own house (*Proverbs 15:27*). He who trusts in his riches will fall. but the righteous will flourish like foliage (*Proverbs 11:28*). Better is a little with righteousness, than vast revenues without justice (*Proverbs 16:8*). Better a handful with quietness than both hands full, together with toil and grasping for the wind (*Ecclesiastes 4:6*). Better a little with the fear of the LORD, than great treasures with trouble. Better is a dinner of herbs where love is, than a fatted calf with hatred (*Proverbs 15:16–17*). And having food and clothing, with these we shall be content (*1 Timothy 6:8*). Seek first the kingdom of God and His righteousness, and all these [necessities] things shall be added to you (*Matthew 6:33*). Let your conduct be without covetousness; be content with such things as you have. For He Himself has said, "I will never leave nor forsake you" (*Hebrews 13:5*). Godliness with contentment is great gain (*1 Timothy 6:6*). The LORD will not allow the righteous soul to famish (*Proverbs 10:3*). Oh, taste and see that the LORD is good; blessed is the man who trusts in Him! Oh, fear the LORD, you His saints! There is no want in those who fear Him (*Psalm 34:9*). But those who seek the LORD shall not lack any good thing (*Psalm 34:10*). Trust in the LORD and do good; dwell in the land and feed on His faithfulness (*Psalm 37:3*). Delight yourself also in the LORD, and He shall give you the desires of your heart (*Psalm 37:4*). The blessing of the LORD makes one rich, and He adds no sorrow with it (*Proverbs 10:22*). He who did not spare His own Son, but delivered Him up for us all, how shall He not with Him also freely give us all things (*Romans 8:32*)?

TO BE ACCEPTABLE IN YOUR SIGHT

Now I [Paul] pray to God that you do no evil,...but that you should do what is honorable (*2 Corinthians 13:7*). That you may walk worthy of the Lord, fully pleasing to Him, being fruitful in every good work and increasing in the knowledge of God; strengthened with all might according to His glorious power, for all patience and longsuffering with joy; giving thanks to the Father who has qualified us to be partakers of the inheritance of the saints in the light (*Colossians 1:10–12*). Let the words of my mouth and the meditation of my heart be acceptable in Your sight, O LORD, my strength and my Redeemer (*Psalm 19:14*). The fear [seeking the approval of] man brings a snare, but whoever trusts in the LORD shall be safe *(Proverbs 29:25)*. Create in me a clean heart, O God, and renew a steadfast spirit within me (*Psalm 51:10*). Let my heart be blameless regarding Your statutes, that I may not be ashamed (*Psalm 119:80*). Therefore we make it our aim, whether present or absent [alive or dead], to be well pleasing to Him [Jesus our Lord] (*2 Corinthians 5:9*). Teach me to do Your will, for you are my God; Your Spirit is good. Lead me in the land of uprightness (*Psalm 143:10*). Search me, O God, and know my heart; try me and know my anxieties; and see if there is any wicked way in me, and lead me in the way everlasting (*Psalm 139:23–24*).

WATCHING OUT FOR WOLVES

"Beware of false prophets, who come to you in sheep's clothing, but inwardly they are ravenous wolves... A good tree cannot bear bad fruit, nor can a bad tree bear good fruit... Therefore by their fruits you will know them" (*Matthew 7:15–20*). Be sober, be vigilant, because your adversary the devil walks about like a roaring lion, seeking whom he may devour. Resist him, steadfast in the faith, knowing that the same sufferings are experienced by your brotherhood in the world (*1 Peter 5:8–9*). In perils among false brethren (*2 Corinthians 11:26*). For such are false apostles, deceitful workers, transforming themselves into apostles of Christ. And no wonder! For Satan himself transforms himself into an angel of light. Therefore it is no great thing if his ministers also transform themselves into ministers of righteousness, whose end will be according to their works (*2 Corinthians 11:13–15*). There were also false prophets among the people, even as there will be false teachers among you, who will secretly bring in destructive heresies, even denying the Lord who bought them, and bring on themselves swift destruction. And many will follow their destructive ways, because of whom the way of truth will be blasphemed. By covetousness they will exploit you with deceptive words; for a long time their judgment has not been idle, and their destruction does not slumber (*2 Peter 2:1–3*). Behold, I send you out as sheep in the midst of wolves. Therefore be wise as serpents and harmless as doves (*Matthew 10:16*).

THE LORD, OUR CHAMPION

Do not be afraid of sudden terror, nor of trouble from the wicked when it comes; for the LORD will be your confidence, and will keep your foot from being caught (*Proverbs 3:25–26*). O LORD, my strength and my fortress, my refuge in the day of affliction (*Jeremiah 16:19*). They [my enemy] confronted me in my calamity, but the LORD was my support (*Psalm 18:18*). Behold, God is my helper; the LORD is with those who uphold my life (*Psalm 54:4*). For I, the LORD your God, will hold your right hand, saying to you, "Fear not, I will help you" (*Isaiah 41:13*). "Blessed are You, LORD God of Israel, our Father forever and ever. Yours, O LORD, is the greatness, the power and the glory, the victory, and the majesty; for all that is in heaven and earth is Yours; Yours is the kingdom, O LORD, and You are exalted as head over all (*1 Chronicles 29:10–11*). Oh, sing to the LORD a new song! For He has done marvelous things, His right hand and His holy arm have gained Him the victory (*Psalm 98:1*). Thanks be to God, who gives us the victory through our Lord Jesus Christ (*1 Corinthians 15:57*).

GREATLY GRATEFUL FOR YOUR WONDEROUS WORKS

We will not hide them from their children, telling to the generation to come the praises of the LORD, and His strength and His wonderful works that He has done (*Psalm 78:4*). One generation shall praise Your works to another, and shall declare Your mighty acts (*Psalm 115:4*). I will meditate on the glorious splendor of Your majesty, and on Your wonderful works. Men shall speak of the might of Your awesome acts, and I will declare Your greatness (*Psalm 145:5–6*). Oh, give thanks to the Lord of lords! For His mercy endures forever. To Him who alone does great wonders, for His mercy endures forever (*Psalm 136:3–4*). Declare His glory among all peoples. For the LORD is great and greatly to be praised (*1 Chronicles 16:24–25*). I thought it good to declare the signs and wonders that the Most High God has worked for me. How great are His signs, and how mighty His wonders! His kingdom is an everlasting kingdom, and His dominion is from generation to generation (*Daniel 4:2–3*).

LOVE, RICH AND EVERLASTING

Love suffers long and is kind; love does not envy; love does not parade itself, is not puffed up.; does not behave rudely, does not seek its own, is not provoked, thinks no evil; does not rejoice in iniquity, but rejoices in the truth; bears all things, believes all things, hopes all things, endures all things. Love never fails (*1 Corinthians 13:4–8*). "The LORD your God in your midst, the Mighty One, will save; He will rejoice over you with gladness, He will quiet you with His love, He will rejoice over you with singing" (*Zephaniah 3:17*). The LORD is gracious and full of compassion, slow to anger and great in mercy (*Psalm 145:8*). But God, who is rich in mercy, because of His great love with which He loved us, even when we were dead in trespasses, made us alive together with Christ [by grace you have been saved], and raised us up together in the heavenly places in Christ Jesus (*Ephesians 2:4–6*). As the Father loved Me, I also have loved you; abide in My love. If you keep My commandments [to love God and others] you will abide in My love, just as I have kept my Father's commandments and abide in His love (*John 15:9–10*). But you, beloved, build yourselves up on your most holy faith, praying in the Holy Spirit, keep yourselves in the love of God, looking for the mercy of our Lord Jesus Christ unto eternal life (*Jude 1:20–21*). "Fear not, for I am with you; be not dismayed, for I am your God. I will strengthen you, yes, I will help you, I will uphold you with My righteous right hand" (*Isaiah 41:10*). Yes, I [God] have loved you with an everlasting love; therefore with loving-kindness I have drawn you (*Jeremiah 31:3*). The God of love and peace be with you (*2 Corinthians 13:11*). The grace of the Lord Jesus Christ, and the love of God, and the communion of the Holy Spirit be with you all. Amen (*2 Corinthians 13:14*).

NOTHING HIDDEN THAT WON'T BE REVEALED

There is no creature hidden from His sight, but all things are naked and open to the eyes of Him to whom we must give account *(Hebrews 4:13)*. The secret things belong to the LORD our God *(Deuteronomy 29:29)*. He reveals deep and secret things; He knows what is in the darkness, and light dwells with Him *(Daniel 2:22)*. And now, Lord, what do I wait for? My hope is in You *(Psalm 39:7)*. "Call to Me, and I will answer you, and show you great and mighty things, which you do not know" *(Jeremiah 33:3)*. His [the LORD's] secret counsel is with the upright *(Proverbs 3:32)*. The secret of the LORD is with those who fear Him, and He will show them His covenant. My eyes are ever toward the LORD, for He shall pluck my feet out of the net *(Psalm 25:14–25)*. But as it is written: "Eye has not seen, nor ear heard, nor have entered into the heart of man the things which God has prepared for those who love Him." But God has revealed them to us through His Spirit. For the Spirit searches all things, yes, the deep things of God *(1 Corinthians 2:9–10)*. Now we have received, not the spirit of the world, but the Spirit who is from God, that we might know the things that have been freely given to us by God *(1 Corinthians 2:12)*. "For nothing is secret that will not be revealed, nor anything hidden that will not be known and come to light" *(Luke 8:17)*. For now we see in a mirror, dimly, but then face to face. Now I know in part, but then I shall now just as I also am known *(1 Corinthians 13:12)*. Beloved, now we are children of God; and it has not yet been revealed what we shall be, but we know that when He is revealed, we shall be like Him, for we shall see Him as He is. And everyone who has this hope in him purifies himself, just as He is pure *(1 John 3:2–3)*. For you were once darkness, but now you are light in the Lord. Walk as children of light (for the fruit of the Spirit is in all goodness, righteousness, and truth), finding out what is acceptable to the Lord *(Ephesians 5:8-10)*. If we walk in the light as He is in the light, we have fellowship with one another, and the blood of Jesus Christ His Son cleanses us from all sin *(1 John 1:7)* Then Jesus spoke to them again, saying, "I am the light of the world. He who follows Me shall not walk in darkness, but have the light of life" *(John 8:12)*.

NOT BEING BENT ON A BAD BARGAIN

Do not be deceived, God is not mocked; for whatever a man sows, that will he also reap. For he who sows to his flesh will of the flesh reap corruption, but he who sows to the Spirit will of the Spirit reap everlasting life (*Ephesians 6:7–8*). Righteousness exalts a nation, but sin is a reproach to any people (*Proverbs 14:34*). The wicked prowl on every side, when vileness is exalted among the sons of men (*Psalm 12:8*). Pride goes before destruction, and a haughty spirit before a fall (*Proverbs 16:18*). An evil man seeks only rebellion; therefore a cruel messenger will be sent against him (*Proverbs 17:11*). For rebellion is as the sin of witchcraft, and stubbornness as iniquity and idolatry (*1 Samuel 15:23*). "Those who regard worthless idols forsake their own mercy" (*Jonah 2:8*). Because the sentence against an evil work is not executed speedily, therefore the heart of the sons of men is fully set in them to do evil (*Ecclesiastes 8:11*). Poverty and shame will come to him who disdains correction, but he who regards a rebuke will be honored (*Proverbs 13:18*). He who disdains instruction despises his own soul, but he who heeds rebuke gets understanding (*Proverbs 15:32*). The highway of the upright is to depart from evil; he who keeps his way preserves his soul (*Proverbs 16:17*). Jesus said to him, "I am the way, the truth, and the life. No one comes to the Father except through Me" *(John 14:6).* "Come now, and let us reason together," says the LORD, "Though your sins are like scarlet, they shall be white as snow; though they are red like crimson, they shall be as wool" *(Isaiah 1:18).*

FOREVER, EVEN FOREVER AND EVER

The eternal God is your refuge and underneath are the everlasting arms (*Deuteronomy 33:27*). For by one offering He has perfected forever those who are being sanctified [set aside for holiness] (*Hebrews 10:14*). Oh, give thanks to the LORD, for He is good! For His mercy endures forever (*Psalm 106:1*). "And this is eternal life, that they may know You, the only true God, and Jesus Christ whom You have sent" (*John 17:3*). And this is the promise that He [God] has promised us—eternal life (*1 John 2:25*). He who believes in Him [Jesus] is not condemned (*John 3:18*). I give them [those who believe] eternal life, and they shall never perish; neither shall anyone snatch them out of My hand (*John 10:28*). And this is the testimony: that God has given us eternal life, and this life is in His Son. He who has the Son has life; he who does not have the Son of God does not have life (*1 John 5:11–13*). That having been justified by His [God's] grace we should become heirs according to the hope of eternal life (*Titus 3:7*). Also I will make Him My firstborn, the highest of the kings of the earth. My mercy I will keep for Him forever, and My covenant shall stand firm with Him. His seed [us who believe in Jesus] also I will make endure forever, and His throne as the days of heaven (*Psalm 89:27–29*). The LORD loves justice, and does not forsake His saints; they are preserved forever (*Psalm 37:28*). The saints of the Most High shall receive the kingdom and possess the kingdom forever, even forever and ever (*Daniel 7:18*). Then the seventh angel sounded: And there were loud voices in heaven saying, "The kingdoms of this world have become the kingdoms of our Lord and of His Christ, and He shall reign forever and ever! (*Revelation 11:15*).

CLEAN COURAGE

A righteous man who falters before the wicked is like a murky spring and a polluted well (*Proverbs 25:26*). Dead flies putrefy the perfumer's ointment, and cause it to give off a foul odor; so does a little folly to one respected for wisdom and honor *(Ecclesiastes 10:1)*. The integrity of the upright will guide them, but the perversity of the unfaithful will destroy them (*Proverbs 11:3*). As for me, You uphold me in my integrity, and set me before Your face forever (*Psalm 41:12*). Let integrity and uprightness preserve me, for I wait for You (*Psalm 25:21*). Vindicate me, O LORD, for I have walked in my integrity. I have also trusted in the LORD; I shall not slip (*Psalm 26:1*). He who walks with integrity walks securely, but he who perverts his ways will become known (*Proverbs 10:9*). He who is faithful in what is least is faithful also in much; and he who is unjust in what is least is unjust also in much (*Luke 16:10*). In all things showing yourself to be a pattern of good works; in doctrine showing integrity, reverence, incorruptibility, sound speech that cannot be condemned, that one who is an opponent may be ashamed, having nothing evil to say of you (*Titus 2:7–8*). And who is he who will harm you if you become followers of what is good? But even if you should suffer for righteousness sake, you are blessed. "And do not be afraid of their threats, nor be troubled." But sanctify the Lord God in your hearts, and always be ready to give a defense to everyone who asks a reason for the hope that is in you, with meekness and fear; having a good conscience, that when they defame you as evildoers, those who revile your good conduct in Christ may be ashamed. For it is better, if it is the will of God, to suffer for doing good than for doing evil (*1 Peter 3:13–17*). Surely He scorns the scornful [Those having contempt for others], but gives grace [strength for courage] to the humble [Those who accurately see themselves and honor others] *(Proverbs 3:34)*.

PRAISE AND PARTAKE OF HIS PERFECT POWER

Who is like You, O LORD, among the gods? Who is like You, glorious in holiness, fearful in praises, doing wonders? *(Exodus 15:11)*. Be exalted, O God above the heavens, and Your glory above all the earth; that Your beloved may be delivered, save with your right hand, and hear me *(Psalm 108:5–6)*. But I will sing of Your power; yes, I will sing aloud of Your mercy in the morning; for You have been my defense and refuge in the day of my trouble. To You, O my strength, I will sing praises; for God is my defense, my God of mercy *(Psalm 59:16–17)*. I will call upon the LORD who is worthy to be praised; so shall I be saved from my enemies *(2 Samuel 22:4* and *Psalm 18:3)*. So I will sing praise to Your name forever, that I may daily perform my vows *(Psalm 61:8)*. Save us, O LORD our God, and gather us among the gentiles, to give thanks to Your holy name, to triumph in Your praise *(Psalm 106:47)*. Let the people praise You, O God; let all the people praise You. Then the earth shall yield her increase; God, our own God, shall bless us, and all the ends of the earth shall fear Him *(Psalm 67:5–7)*. My heart is steadfast, O God, my heart is steadfast; I will sing and give praise *(Psalm 57:7)*. He has put a new song in my mouth -- Praise to our God; many will see it and fear, and will trust in the LORD *(Psalm 40:3)*.

PRESERVED AND GUARDED IN CHRIST

To those who are called, sanctified by God the Father, and preserved in Jesus Christ (*Jude 1:1*). To an inheritance incorruptible and undefiled and that does not fade away, reserved in heaven for you, who are kept by the power of God through faith for salvation ready to be revealed in the last time *(1 Peter 1:4–5)*. Preserve me, O God, for in You I put my trust (*Psalm 16:1*). Do not withhold Your tender mercies from me, O LORD; let Your loving-kindness and Your truth preserve me (*Psalm 40:11*). You are my hiding place; You shall preserve me from trouble (*Psalm 32:7*). The LORD shall preserve you from all evil; He shall preserve your soul. The LORD shall preserve your going out and your coming in from this time forth, and even forevermore (*Psalm 121:7–8*). The Lord is faithful, who will establish you and guard you from the evil one (*2 Thessalonians 3:3*). For the LORD loves justice, and does not forsake His saints; they are preserved forever (*Psalm 37:28*). Oh, love the LORD, all you His saints! For the LORD preserves the faithful *(Psalm 31:23)*. The Lord will deliver me from every evil work and preserve me for His heavenly kingdom. To Him be glory for ever and ever. Amen! (*2 Timothy 4:18*). Now may the God of peace Himself sanctify you completely; and may your whole spirit, soul, and body be preserved blameless at the coming of our Lord Jesus Christ. He who calls you is faithful, who will also do it (*2 Thessalonians 5:23–24*).

SHIELDING AND SHELTERING SAVIOR

O Lord our shield (*Psalm 59:11*). Deliver me, O LORD, from my enemies; in you I take shelter (*Psalm 143:9*). You are my hiding place and my shield; I hope in Your word (*Psalm 119:114*). Every word of God is pure; He is a shield to those who put their trust in Him (*Proverbs 30:5*). The LORD will be a shelter for His people, and the strength of the children of Israel (*Joel 3:16*). For You, O LORD, will bless the righteous; with favor You will surround him as with a shield (*Psalm 5:12*). You have also given me the shield of Your salvation; Your gentleness has made me great. You enlarge my path under me; so my feet did not slip (*2 Samuel 22:36–37*). His truth shall be your shield and buckler [small shield worn on the forearm] (*Psalm 91:4*). For the shields of the earth belong to God, He is greatly exalted (*Psalm 47:9*). The LORD is my strength and my shield; my heart trusted in Him, and I am helped; therefore my heart greatly rejoices, and with my song I will praise Him (*Psalm 28:7*). For You have been a shelter for me, a strong tower from the enemy (*Psalm 61:3*). "Do not be afraid, Abram. I am your shield, your exceedingly great reward" (*Genesis 15:1*). But you, O LORD, are a shield for me, my glory and the One who lifts up my head (*Psalm 3:3*). Our soul waits for the LORD; He is our help and our shield (*Psalm 33:20*). For the LORD is a sun and a shield; the LORD will give grace and glory; no good thing will He withhold from those who walk uprightly. O LORD of hosts, blessed is the man who trusts in You! (*Psalm 84:11–12*). Above all, taking the shield of faith with which you will be able to quench all the fiery darts of the wicked one (*Ephesians 6:16*). For we know that if our earthly house, this tent, is destroyed, we have a building from God, a house not made with hands, eternal in the heavens *(2 Corinthians 5:1)*.

THE LORD OUR RIGHTEOUSNESS

To those who have obtain like precious faith with us by the righteousness of our God and savior Jesus Christ (*2 Peter 1:1*). Even the righteousness of God, through faith in Jesus Christ, to all and on all who believe *(Romans 3:22)*. Christ is the end of the law for righteousness to everyone who believes (*Romans 10:4*). That I may gain Christ and be found in Him, not having my own righteousness, which is from the law, but that which is by faith in Christ, the righteousness which is from God by faith (*Philippians 3:8–9*). For He [God the Father] made Him [Jesus His Son] who knew no sin to be sin for us, that we might become the righteousness of God in Him (*2 Corinthians 5:21*). Now this is His name by which He will be called: THE LORD OUR RIGHTEOUSNESS (*Jeremiah 23:6*). For the LORD is righteous, He loves righteousness; His countenance beholds the upright (*Psalm 11:7*). The LORD knows the days of the upright, and their inheritance shall be forever. They shall not be ashamed in the evil time, and in the days of famine they shall be satisfied (*Psalm 37:18–19*). The salvation of the righteous is from the LORD; He is their strength in the time of trouble. And the LORD shall help them and deliver them; You will deliver them from the wicked, and save them, because they trust in Him (*Psalm 37:39–40*). The righteous has an everlasting foundation (*Proverbs 10:25*). My mouth shall tell of Your righteousness and Your salvation all the day, for I know not their limits. I will go in the strength of the Lord GOD; I will make mention of Your righteousness, of Yours only (*Psalm 71:15–16*).

PARTAKING IN HIS PROMISES

The scripture has confined all under sin, that the promise by faith in Jesus Christ might be given to those who believe (*Galatians 3:22*). And if you are Christ's, then you are Abraham's seed, and heirs according to the promise (*Galatians 3:29*). That the gentiles should be fellow heirs, of the same body, and partakers of His [God's] promise in Christ through the gospel (*Galatians 3:6*). Grace and peace be multiplied to you in the knowledge of God and of Jesus Christ our Lord, as His divine power has given to us all things that pertain to life and godliness, through the knowledge of Him who called us to glory and virtue, by which is given to us exceedingly great and precious promises, that through these you may be partakers of the divine nature, having escaped the corruption that is in the world through lust (*2 Peter 1:2–4*). Inasmuch as He [Jesus Christ our High Priest] is also mediator [the one who brings us together with God] of a better covenant, which is established on better promises (*Hebrews 8:6*). For all the promises of God in Him [Jesus] are yes, and in Him Amen, to the glory of God through us (*2 Corinthians 1:20*). Therefore, having these promises, beloved, let us cleanse ourselves from all filthiness of the flesh and spirit, perfecting holiness in the fear of God (*2 Corinthians 7:1*). And we desire that each one of you show the same diligence to the full assurance of hope until the end, that you do not become sluggish, but imitate those who through faith and patience inherit the promises. For when God made a promise to Abraham, because He could swear by no one greater, He swore by Himself, saying, "Surely blessing I will bless you, and multiplying I will multiply you." And so, after he had patiently endured, he obtained the promise (*Hebrews 6:12–15*). For you have need of endurance, so that after you have done the will of God, you may receive the promise (*Hebrews 10:36*). Thus God, determining to show more abundantly to the heirs of the promise the immutability [not able to be changed] of His counsel, confirmed it by an oath (*Hebrews 6:17*). God is faithful, by whom you were called into fellowship of His Son, Jesus Christ our Lord (*1 Corinthians 1:9*). All that the Father gives Me [Jesus] will come to Me, and the one who comes to Me I will by no means cast out (*John 6:37*). That those who are called may receive the promise of the eternal inheritance (*Hebrews 9:15*). And this is the promise that He [God] has promised us—eternal life (*1 John 2:25*).

LEANING ON THE LORD LIGHTS THE WAY

The LORD is my light and my salvation (*Psalm 27:1*). For with You is the fountain of life; in Your light we see light (*Psalm 37:9*). Oh, send out Your light and Your truth! Let them lead me (*Psalm 43:3*). Your word is a lamp to my feet and a light to my path (*Psalm 119:105*). The light of the righteous rejoices, but the lamp of the wicked will be put out (*Proverbs 13:9*). Unto the upright there arises light in the darkness (*Psalm 112:4*). Do all things without murmuring and disputing, that you may become blameless and harmless children of God without fault in the midst of a crooked and perverse generation, among whom you shine as lights in the world (*Philippians 2:16–17*). Light is sown for the righteous, and gladness for the upright in heart (*Psalm 97:11*). Who among you fears the Lord? Who obeys the voice of His servant? Who walks in darkness and has no light? Let him trust in the name of the Lord and rely upon His God (*Isaiah 50:10*). Commit your way to the LORD, trust also in Him, and He shall bring it to pass. He shall bring forth your righteousness as the light, and your justice as the noonday (*Psalm 37:5–6*). "I [Jesus] am the light of the world. He who follows Me shall not walk in darkness, but have the light of life (*John 8:12*). For now we see in a mirror, dimly, but then face to face. Now I know in part, but then I shall know just as I am known. And now abide faith, hope, love, these three; but the greatest of these is love (*1 Corinthians 13:12-13*).

DIVINELY DRAWN

Draw near to my soul and redeem it (*Psalm 69:18*). I wanted to gather your children together, as a hen gathers her chicks under her wings, but you were not willing (*Matthew 23:37*). Does not wisdom cry out, and understanding lift up her voice? "Listen, for I will speak excellent things" (*Proverbs 8:1 and 6*). Draw near to hear rather than to give the sacrifice of fools (*Ecclesiastes 5:1*). Draw near to God and He will draw near to you (*James 4:8*). It is good for me to draw near to God; I have put my trust in the Lord GOD, that I may declare all Your works (*Psalm 73:28*). For He [Jesus] Himself has said, I will never leave you nor forsake you (*Hebrews 13:5*). There is the bringing in of a better hope [Jesus our Savior], through which we draw near to God (*Hebrews 7:19*). "And I [Jesus], if I am lifted up from the earth [crucified on the cross], will draw all peoples to Myself" (*John 12:32*). No one can come to me unless the Father who sent me draws him; and I will raise him up at the last day (*John 6:44*). Let us draw near with a true heart in full assurance of faith, having our hearts sprinkled from an evil conscience and our bodies washed with pure water. Let us hold fast the confession of our hope without wavering, for He [God] who promised is faithful (*Hebrews 10:22*). They shall call them Holy people, the redeemed of the LORD; and you shall be called sought out and not forsaken (*Isaiah 62:12*). Yes, I have loved you with an everlasting love; therefore with loving-kindness I have drawn you (*Jeremiah 31:3*).

ACCEPTING ALTERATIONS

He who instructs the nations, shall He not correct (*Psalm 94:10*). A wise son heeds his father's instruction, but a scoffer does not listen to rebuke (*Proverbs 13:1*). A scoffer does not love one who corrects him, nor will he go to the wise (*Proverbs 15:12*). Whoever loves instruction loves knowledge, but he who hates correction is stupid (*Proverbs 12:1*). He who disdains instruction despises his own soul, but he who heeds rebuke gets understanding (*Proverbs 15:32*). The ear that hears the rebukes of life will abide among the wise (*Proverbs 15:31*). A fool despises his father's instruction. He who receives correction is prudent [careful in living appropriately and avoiding trouble] (*Proverbs 15:5*). Poverty and shame will come to him who disdains correction, but he who regards a rebuke will be honored (*Proverbs 13:18*). O God, You know my foolishness; and my sins are not hidden from You (*Psalm 69:5*). Your word I have hidden in my heart, that I might not sin against You (*Psalm 119:11*). Let the words of my mouth and the meditations of my heart be acceptable in Your sight, O LORD, my strength and redeemer (*Psalm 19:14*).

PROBLEMATIC BUT PROTECTED PEOPLE

But we have this treasure in earthen vessels, that the excellence of the power may be of God and not of us. We are hard pressed on every side, yet not crushed; we are perplexed, but not in despair; persecuted, but not forsaken; struck down, but not destroyed—always carrying about in the body the dying of the Lord Jesus Christ, that the life of Jesus also may be manifest in our body (*2 Corinthians 4:7–9*). To establish you and encourage you concerning you concerning your faith, that no one should be shaken by these afflictions; for you yourselves know that we are appointed to this. For in fact, we told you before when we were with you that we would suffer tribulation, just as it happened, and you know (*1 Thessalonians 3:2–4*). I will cry out to God Most High, to God who performs all things for me; He shall send from heaven and save me; He reproaches the one who would swallow me up. God shall send forth His mercy and His truth (*Psalm 57:2–3*). Through God we will do valiantly, for it is He who shall tread down our enemies (*Psalm 60:12*). The wicked watches the righteous, and seeks to slay him. The LORD will not leave him in his hand, nor condemn him when he is judged (*Psalm 37:32–33*). But the Lord is faithful, who will establish you and guard you from the evil one (*2 Thessalonians 3:3*). When the enemy comes in like a flood, the Spirit of the LORD will lift up a standard against him (*Isaiah 59:19*). You will be betrayed even by parents and brothers, relatives and friends; they will put some of you to death. And you will be hated by all for My name's sake. But not a hair on your head shall be lost. By your patience possess your souls (*Luke 21:16–18*). For I consider that the sufferings of this present time are not worthy to be compared with the glory which shall be revealed in us (*Romans 8:18*). "My sheep hear My voice, and I [Jesus] know them, and they follow Me. And I give them eternal life, and they shall never perish; neither shall anyone snatch them out of My hand" (*John 10:27–28*).

PUTTING OUR LOVE TO WORK

For God is not unjust to forget your work and labor of love which you have shown toward His name, in that you have ministered to the saints and do minister (*Hebrews 6:10*). I have been shown in every way, by laboring like this, that you must support the weak. And remember the words of the Lord Jesus, that He said, "It is more blessed to give than to receive" (*Acts 20:35*). And God is able to make all grace abound toward you, that you, always having all sufficiency in all things, may have an abundance for every good work (*2 Corinthians 9:8*). But do not forget to do good and to share, for with such sacrifices God is well pleased (*Hebrews 13:16*). But as for you, brethren, do not grow weary in doing good (*2 Thessalonians 3:13*). This is a faithful saying, and these things I [Paul the apostle] want you to affirm constantly, that those who believe in God should be careful to maintain good works. These things are good and profitable to men (*Titus 3:8*). And let our people also learn to maintain good works, to meet urgent needs, that they may not be unfruitful (*Titus 3:14*). And let us not grow while doing good, for in due season we shall reap if we do not lose heart. Therefore, as we you have opportunity, let us do good to all, especially to those who are of the household of faith (*Galatians 6:9*), distributing to the needs of the saints, given to hospitality (*Romans 12:13*). Beloved, you do faithfully whatever you do for the brethren and for strangers (*3 John 1:5*). My little children, let us not love in word or in tongue, but in deed and in truth (*1 John 3:18*).

LORD GOD, ROCK OF LIFE

To You I will cry, O LORD my Rock: Do not be silent to me, lest, if you are silent to me, I become like those who go down to the pit (*Psalm 28:1*). Bow down your ear to me, deliver me speedily; be my rock of refuge, a fortress of defense to save me (*Psalm 31:2*). Do not fear, nor be afraid; have I not told you from that time, and declared it? You are My witnesses. Is there a God besides Me? Indeed there is no other Rock; I know not one (*Isaiah 44:8*). No one is holy like the LORD, for there is none besides You, nor is there any rock like our God (*1 Samuel 2:2*). He is the Rock, His work is perfect; for all His ways are justice, a God of truth and without injustice; righteous and upright is He (*Deuteronomy 32:4*). "The LORD is my rock and my fortress and my deliverer" (*2 Samuel 22:2*). I will love You, O LORD, my strength. The LORD is my rock and my fortress and my deliverer; my God, my strength, in whom I trust; my shield and the horn of my salvation, my stronghold (*Psalm 18:1–2*). For who is God, except the LORD? And who is a rock, except our God? (*2 Samuel 22:32* and *Psalm 18:31*). The LORD has been my defense, and my God the rock of my refuge (*Psalm 94:22*). The LORD lives! Blessed be my rock! Let God be exalted, the rock of my salvation! (*2 Samuel 22:47*). When my heart is overwhelmed; lead me to the rock that is high than I (*Psalm 61:2*). The Lord lives! Blessed be my rock! Let the God of my salvation be exalted (*Psalm 18:46*). A man will be a hiding place from the wind, and a cover from the tempest, as rivers of water in a dry place, as the shadow of a great rock in a weary land (*Isaiah 32:2*). Therefore thus says the Lord God: "Behold I lay in Zion a stone for a foundation, a tried stone, a precious cornerstone, a sure foundation; whoever believes will not act hastily" (*Isaiah 28:16*). Therefore whoever hears these sayings of mine, and does them, I [Jesus] will liken him to a wise man who built his house on the rock (*Matthew 7:24*). Oh come, let us sing to the LORD! Let us shout joyfully to the Rock of our salvation (*Psalm 95:1*). The righteous shall flourish like a palm tree, he shall grow like a cedar in Lebanon. Those who are planted in the house of the LORD shall flourish in the courts of our God. They shall still bear fruit in old age; they shall be fresh and flourishing, to declare that the LORD is upright; He is my rock, and there is no unrighteousness in Him (*Psalm 92:12–15*).

FRIEND OR FOE, FOREWARNED IS FOREARMED

O LORD my God, in You I put my trust; save me from all those who persecute me; and deliver me *(Psalm 7:1)*. "But watch out for yourselves, for they will deliver you up to the councils, and you will be beaten in the synagogues. You will be brought before rulers and kings for My sake, for a testimony to them" *(Mark 13:9)*. But as he who was born according to the flesh then persecuted him who was born according to the Spirit, even so it is now *(Galatians 4:29)*. An unjust man is an abomination to the righteous, and he who is upright in the way is an abomination to the wicked *(Proverbs 29:27)*. "And a man's enemies will be those of his own household *(Matthew 10:36)*. For it is not an enemy who reproaches me; then I could bear it. Nor is it one who hates me who has exalted himself against me; then I could hide myself from him. But it was you, a man my equal, my companion and my acquaintance. We took sweet counsel together, and walked to the house of God in the throng *(Psalm 55:12–14)*. Even my own familiar friend in whom I trusted, who ate bread my bread, has lifted his heel against me *(Psalm 41:9)*. In return for my love they are my accusers, but I give myself to prayer. Thus they have rewarded me evil for good, and hatred for my love *(Psalm 109:4–5)*. "Yes, the time is coming that whoever kills you will think he offers God service. And these things they will do to you because they have not known the Father nor Me" *(John 16:2–3)*. "Blessed are you when they revile and persecute you, and say all kinds of evil against you falsely for My sake. Rejoice and be exceedingly glad, for great is your reward in heaven, for so they persecuted the prophets who were before you" *(Matthew 5:11–12)*. "I [Jesus, God's Son] say to you, love your enemies, bless those who curse you, do good to those who hate you, and pray for those who spitefully use you and persecute you, that you may be sons of your Father in heaven; for He makes His sun rise on the evil and on the good and sends rain on the just and on the unjust (*Matthew 5:44–45*). Repay no one evil for evil. Have regard for good things in the sight of all men. Beloved, do not avenge yourselves, but rather give place to wrath; for it is written, "Vengeance is Mine, I will repay," says the Lord (*Romans 12:17–19*). If your enemy is hungry, give him bread to eat; and if he is thirsty, give him water to drink; for so you will heap coals of fire on His head, and the LORD will reward you (*Proverbs 25:21–22*). I [the Apostle Paul] know whom [the Lord Jesus] I have believed and am persuaded that He is able to keep what I have committed to Him until that day (*2 Timothy 1:12*). Therefore do not be ashamed of the testimony of our Lord, nor of me [Paul] His prisoner, but share with me in the sufferings for the gospel according to the power of God (*2 Timothy 1:8*). Do not be overcome by evil, but overcome evil with good (*Romans 12:21*). Therefore take up the whole armor of God, that you may be able to stand in the evil day, and having done all, to stand. Stand therefore (*Ephesians 6:13–14*). For your patience and faith in all your persecutions and tribulations that you endure, which is manifest evidence of the righteous judgment of God, that you may be counted worthy of the kingdom of God, for which you also suffer; since it is a righteous thing with God to repay with tribulation those who trouble you, and to give you who are troubled rest with us when the Lord Jesus is revealed from heaven with His mighty angels *(2 Thessalonians 1:4–7)*.

OH, THAT GOD'S PEOPLE WOULD PRAISE HIM!

Oh, bless our God you peoples! And make the voice of His praise to be heard (*Psalm 66:8*). Those who seek Him will praise the LORD (*Psalm 22:26*). Then they believed His word; they sang His praise (*Psalm 106:12*). This people I have formed for Myself; they shall declare My praise (*Isaiah 43:21*). All Your works shall praise You, O LORD, and Your saints shall bless You. *(Psalm 145:10)* You who fear the LORD praise Him *(Psalm 22:23)*. Praise the LORD from the earth, kings of the earth and all peoples; princes and all judges of the earth; both young men and maidens; old men and children (*Psalm 148:7, 11–12*). Great is the LORD, and greatly to be praised; and His greatness is unsearchable (*Psalm 145:3*). Praise the LORD! For it is good to sing praises to our God; for it is pleasant, and praise is beautiful (*Psalm 147:1*). Give unto the LORD the glory due to His name; worship the LORD in the beauty of holiness (*Psalm 29:2*). Exalt the LORD our God, and worship at His holy hill; for the LORD our God is holy (*Psalm 99:9*). For the Lord is the King of all the earth; sing praises with understanding (*Psalm 47:7*). Let heaven and earth praise Him, the seas and everything in them (*Psalm 69:34*). And in His temple everyone says, "Glory!" (*Psalm 29:9*). Blessed be the LORD God of Israel from everlasting to everlasting! And let all the people say, Amen! Praise the LORD! (*Psalm 106:48*). O LORD, our Lord, how excellent is Your name in all the earth, who have set Your glory above the heavens! (*Psalm 8:1*). Be exalted, O God, above the heavens; let Your glory be above all the earth (*Psalm 57:5*). I will declare Your name to my brethren; in the midst of the assembly I will praise You (*Psalm 22:22*). I will praise You, O Lord my God, with all my heart, and I will glorify Your name forevermore. For great is Your mercy toward me, and You have delivered my soul from Sheol [Hades] *(Psalm 86:12–13)*. "Whoever offers praise glorifies Me; and to him who orders His conduct aright I will show the salvation of God" *(Psalm 50:23)*. Therefore by Him [Jesus] let us continually offer the sacrifice of praise to God, that is, the fruit of our lips, giving thanks to His name *(Hebrews 13:15)*.

HUNGERING FOR THE RIGHT THINGS

Why do you spend money for what is not bread, and your wages for what does not satisfy? Listen carefully to Me, and eat what is good, and let your soul delight itself in abundance. Incline your ear, and come to Me. Hear and your soul shall live (*Isaiah 55:23*). Blessed are those who hunger and thirst for righteousness, for they shall be filled (*Matthew 5:6*). For He satisfies the longing soul, and fills the hungry soul with goodness (*Psalm 107:9*). Blessed are you who hunger now, for you shall be filled (*Luke 6:21*). He has filled the hungry with good things (*Luke 1:53*). He makes peace in your borders, and fills you with the finest wheat (*Psalm 147:14*). The righteous eats to the satisfying of his soul (*Proverbs 13:25*). I spread out my hands to You; my soul longs for You like a thirsty land (*Psalm 143:6*). How lovely is your tabernacle, O LORD of hosts! My soul longs, yes, even faints for the courts of the LORD; my heart and my flesh cry out for the living God (*Psalm 84:1–2*). As the deer pants for the water brooks, so pants my soul for You, O God. My soul thirsts for God, for the living God *(Psalms 42:1-2)*. The LORD is gracious and full of compassion. He has given food to those who fear Him (*Psalm 111:4–5*). Blessed is the man you choose, and cause to approach you, that He may dwell in your courts. We shall be satisfied with the goodness of Your house, of Your holy temple (*Psalm 65:4*). For the needy will not always be forgotten; the expectation of the poor shall not perish forever (*Psalm 9:18*). "My people shall be satisfied with My goodness, says the LORD" (*Jeremiah 31:14*). How precious is Your loving-kindness, O God! Therefore the children of men put their trust under the shadow of Your wings. They are abundantly satisfied with the fullness of Your house, and You give them drink from the river of Your pleasures. For with You is the fountain of life; in Your light we see light (*Psalm 36:7–9*). You prepare a table before me in the presents of my enemies; You anoint my head with oil; my cup runs over (*Psalm 23:5*). Jesus said to them, "I am the bread of life. He who comes to Me shall never hunger, and he who believes in Me shall never thirst" (*John 6:35*).

INCLUDING THANKSGIVING IN AND FOR EVERYTHING

It is good to give thanks to the LORD, and to sing praises to Your name, O Most High (*Psalm 92:1*). I will offer to You the sacrifice of thanksgiving, and will call upon the name of the LORD (*Psalm 116:17*). Surely the righteous shall give thanks to Your name; the upright shall dwell in Your presence (*Psalm 140:13*). Oh, that men would give thanks to the LORD for His goodness, and for His wonderful works to the children of men! Let them sacrifice the sacrifices of thanks giving, and declare His works with rejoicing (*Psalm 107:21-22*). We give thanks to the God and Father of our Lord Jesus Christ, praying always for you (*Colossians 1:3*). Continue earnestly in prayer, being vigilant in it with thanksgiving (*Colossians 4:2*). Offer to God thanksgiving, and pay your vows to the Most High (*Psalm 50:14*). Enter into His gates with thanksgiving, and into His courts with praise (*Psalm 100:4*). "And when you offer a sacrifice of thanksgiving to the LORD, offer it of your own free will" (*Leviticus 22:29*). And whatever you do in word or deed, do all in the name of the Lord Jesus, giving thanks to God the Father through Him (*Colossians 3:17*). Oh, give thanks to the LORD! Call upon His name; make known His deeds among the peoples! (*Psalm 105:1*). I will give thanks in the great assembly; I will praise You among many people (*Psalm 35:18*). Let us come before His presence with thanksgiving; let us shout joyfully to Him with psalms (*Psalm 95:2*). Sing to the LORD with thanksgiving (*Psalm147:7*). At midnight I will rise to give thanks to You, because of Your righteous judgments (*Psalm 119:62*). Oh, give thanks to the LORD, for He is good! For His mercy endures forever (*Psalm 107:1; 118:1, 29;*

and *1 Chronicles 16:34*). So we, Your people and the sheep of Your pasture, will give You thanks forever; we will show forth Your praise to all generations (*Psalm 79:13*). Be anxious for nothing, but in everything by prayer and supplication, with thanksgiving, let your requests be known to God; and the peace of God, which passes all understanding, will guard your hearts and minds through Christ Jesus (*Philippians 4:6–7*). In everything give thanks; for this is the will of God in Christ Jesus for you (*1 Thessalonians 5:18*). Giving thanks always for all things to God the Father in the name of our Lord Jesus Christ (*Ephesians 5:20*). Therefore by Him let us continually offer the sacrifice of praise to God, that is the fruit of our lips, giving thanks to His name (*Hebrews 13:15*).

BEING RETURN READY

"Break up the fallow [left dormant and unsown] ground, and do not sow among thorns. Circumcise yourselves to the LORD, and take away the foreskins of your hearts" (*Jeremiah 4:4*). "Because you say, I am rich, have become wealthy, and have need of nothing—and do not know that you are wretched, miserable, poor, blind and naked—I counsel you to buy from Me gold refined in fire, that you may be rich; and white garments, that you may be clothed, that the shame of your nakedness may not be revealed; and anoint your eyes with eye salve, that you may see" (*Revelation 3:17–18*). This same Jesus, who was taken up from you into heaven, will so come in like manner as you saw Him go into heaven" *(Acts 1:11)*. And behold, I am coming quickly, and My reward is with Me, to give everyone according to his work (*Revelation 22:12*). "Take heed, watch and pray, for you do not know when the time is" (*Mark 13:33*). "Watch therefore, for you do not know when the master of the house [Christ] is coming—in the evening, at midnight, at the crowing of the rooster, or in the morning—lest, coming suddenly, he find you sleeping. And what I say to you, I say to all: Watch!" (*Mark 13:35–37*). "But take heed to yourselves, lest your hearts be weighed down with carousing, drunkenness, and cares of this life, and that day come on you unexpectedly. For it will come as a snare on all those who dwell on the face of the earth. Watch therefore, and pray always that you may be counted worthy to escape all these things that will come to pass, and to stand before the Son of Man" (*Luke 21:34–36*). In My Father's house are many mansions; if it were not so, I would have told you. I go to prepare a place for you. And if I go and prepare a place for you, I will come again and receive you to Myself; that where I am, there you may be also *(John 14:2–3)*. And now, little children, abide in Him, that when He appears, we may have confidence and not be ashamed before Him at His coming (*1 John 2:28*). Let your waist be girded and your lamps burning; and you yourselves be like men who wait for their master, when he will return from the wedding, that when he comes and knocks they may open to him immediately (*Luke 12:35-36*).He [Jesus] who testifies to these things says, "Surely I am coming quickly" Amen. Even so, come, Lord Jesus! The grace of our Lord Jesus Christ be with you all. Amen (*Revelation 22:20–21*).

LOVED BY THE FATHER AND THE SON. AMEN!

The LORD will not cast off His people, nor will He forsake His inheritance (*Psalm 94:14*). "Yes, I have loved you with an everlasting love" (*Jeremiah 31:3*). Behold what manner of love the Father has bestowed on us, that we should be called children of God! (*1 John 3:1*). If anyone loves Me [Jesus], he will keep My word; and My Father will love him, and we will come to him and make Our home with him (*John 14:23*). Having loved His own who were in the world, He will love them to the end (*John 13:1*). Jesus Christ is the same yesterday, today, and forever (*Hebrews 13:8*). Grace, mercy, and peace will be with you from God the Father and from the Lord Jesus Christ, the Son of the Father, in truth and love (*2 John 1:3*). "For the Father Himself loves you, because you have loved Me, and have believed that I came forth from God" (*John 16:27*). But God, who is rich in mercy, because of His great love with which He loved us, even when we were dead in trespasses, made us alive together with Christ [by grace you have been saved], and raised us up together, and made us sit together in the heavenly places in Christ Jesus, that in the ages to come He might show the exceeding riches of His grace in His kindness toward us in Christ Jesus (*Ephesians 2:4–7*). That their hearts may be encouraged, being knit together in love, and attaining to all the riches of full assurance of understanding, to the knowledge of the mystery of God, both of the Father and of Christ (*Colossians 2:2*). He who did not spare His own Son, but delivered Him up for us all, how shall He not with Him also freely give us all things? (*Romans 8:32*). Peace to the brethren, and love with faith, from God the Father and the Lord Jesus Christ. Grace be with all those who love our Lord

Jesus Christ in sincerity. Amen (*Ephesians 6:23–24*). Now may our Lord Jesus Christ Himself, and our God and Father, who has loved us and given us everlasting consolation and good hope by grace, comfort your hearts and establish you in every good word and work (*2 Thessalonians 2:16–17*).

NO SHAME IN SERVING

"When you are invited by anyone to a wedding feast, do not sit down in the best place, lest one more honorable than you be invited by him; and he who invited you and him come and say to you, 'Give place to this man,' and you begin with shame to take the lowest place. But when you are invited, go and sit down in the lowest place, so when he who invited you comes he may say to you, 'Friend, go up higher,' then you will have glory in the presence of those who sit at table. For whoever exalts himself will be humbled, and he who humbles himself will be exalted" (*Luke 14:8–11*). For you see your calling brethren, that not many wise according to the flesh, not many mighty, not many noble, are called. But God has chosen the foolish things of the world to put to shame the wise, and God has chosen the weak things of the world to put to shame the things that are mighty; And the base things of the world and the things that are despised God has chosen, and the things which are not, to bring to nothing the things that are, that no flesh should glory in the presence (*2 Corinthians 1:26–29*). "You know that the rulers of the gentiles lord it over them, and those who are great exercise authority over them. Yet it shall not be so among you; but whoever desires to be great among you, let him be your servant. And whoever desires to be first among you, let Him be your slave—just as the Son of Man did not come to be served, but to serve, and to give His life a ransom for many" (*Matthew 20:25–28*). "But he who is greatest among you shall be your servant. And whoever exalts himself will be humbled, and he who humbles himself will be exalted" (*Matthew 23:11–12*). So when He [Jesus] had washed their feet, taken His garments, and sat down again, He said to them, "Do you know what I have done to you? You call Me teacher and Lord, and you say well, for so I am. If

I then your Lord and teacher, have washed your feet, you also ought to wash one another's feet. For I have given you an example, that you should do as I have done to you. Most assuredly, I say to you, a servant is not greater than his master; nor is he who is sent greater than he who sent him. If you know these things, blessed are you if you do them (*John 13:12–17*).

PRAYER, MORE THAN A PLUS

Be anxious for nothing, but in everything by prayer and supplication, with thanksgiving, let your requests be made known to God; and the peace of God, which surpasses all understanding, will guard your hearts and minds through Christ Jesus (*Philippians 4:6–7*). He [Jesus] spoke a parable to them, that men always ought to pray and not lose heart (*Luke 18:1*). He [Jesus] Himself often withdrew into the wilderness and prayed (*Luke 5:16*). Now it came to pass in those days that He went out into the mountain to pray and continued all night in prayer to God (*Luke 6:12*). Now in the morning, having risen a long while before daylight, He went out and departed to a solitary place; and there He prayed (*Mark 1:35*). Therefore I exhort first of all that supplications, prayers, intercessions, and giving of thanks be made for all men, for kings and all who are in authority, that we may live a quiet and peaceable life in all godliness and reverence. For this is good and acceptable in the sight of God our Savior, who desires all men to be saved and to come to the knowledge of the truth (*1 Timothy 2:1–4*). He [God] shall regard the prayer of the destitute, and shall not despise their prayer (*Psalm 102:17*). And whenever you stand praying, If you have anything against anyone, forgive him, that your Father in heaven may also forgive you your trespasses (*Mark 11:25*). Then you will call upon Me [God] and go and pray to Me, and I will listen to you. And you will seek me and find Me, when you search for Me with all your heart (*Jeremiah 29:12–13*). Continue earnestly in prayer, being vigilant in it with thanksgiving (*Colossians 4:2*). Praying always with all prayer and supplication in the Spirit, being watchful to this end with all perseverance and supplication for all the saints (*Ephesians 6:18*). "Watch and pray, lest you enter into temptation" (*Matthew 26:41*). But you, beloved, building yourselves up on your most holy faith, praying in the Holy Spirit, keep yourselves in the love of God, looking for the mercy of our Lord Jesus Christ unto eternal life (*Jude 1:20–21*). I [Jesus] say to you, love your enemies, bless those who curse you, do good to those who hate you, and pray for those who spitefully use you and persecute you, that you may be sons of your Father in heaven (*Matthew 5:44–45*). He [Jesus Christ] is also able to save to the uttermost those who come to God through Him, since He always lives to make intercession for them (*Hebrews 7:25*). "But you, when you pray, go into your room, and when you have shut the door, pray to your Father who is in the secret place; and your Father who sees in secret will reward you openly (*Matthew 6:6*). "And whatever things you ask in prayer, believing, you will receive" (*Matthew 21:22*). "And whatever you ask in My name, that will I do, that the Father may be glorified in the Son. If you ask anything in My name, I will do it (*John 14:13–14*). Pray without ceasing (*1 Thessalonians 5:17*). If My people who are called by My name will humble themselves, and pray and seek My face, and turn from their wicked ways, then I will hear from heaven, and will forgive their sin and heal their land *(2 Chronicles 7:14)*. But the end of all things is at hand; therefore be serious and watchful in your prayers (*1 Peter 4:7*).

ABUNDANT REDEMPTION

Lift up your eyes to the heavens, and look to the earth beneath. The earth will grow old like a garment, and those who dwell in it will die in like manner; but My salvation will be forever (*Isaiah 51:6*). For with the LORD there is mercy, and with Him abundant redemption (*Psalm 130:7*). Not with the blood of goats and calves, but with His own blood He entered the Most Holy Place once for all, having obtained eternal redemption (*Hebrews 9:12*). And having been perfected, He became the author of eternal salvation to all who obey Him (*Hebrews 5:9*). "I [God the Father] will also give You [Jesus His Son] as a light to the gentiles [non-Jewish people], that You should be My salvation to the ends of the earth" (*Isaiah 49:6*). For I [Paul] am not ashamed of the gospel [good news] of Christ, for it is the power of God to salvation for everyone who believes, for the Jew first and also for the Greek [Greek and other non-Jews] (*Romans 1:16*). Nor is there salvation in any other, for there is no other name under heaven given among men by which we must be saved (*Acts 4:12*). For God did not appoint us to wrath, but to obtain salvation through our Lord Jesus Christ (*1 Thessalonians 5:9*), being justified freely by His grace through the redemption that is in Christ Jesus (*Romans 3:24*). But we are bound to give thanks to God always for you, brethren beloved of the Lord, because God from the beginning chose you for salvation through sanctification by the Spirit and belief in the truth, to which He called you by our gospel, for the obtaining of the glory of our Lord Jesus Christ (*2 Thessalonians 2:13–14*). In Him [the Lord Jesus] you also trusted, after you heard the word of truth, the gospel of your salvation; in whom also, having believed, you were sealed with the Holy Spirit of promise, who is the guarantee of our inheritance until the redemption of the purchased possession, to the praise of

His glory (*Ephesians 1:13–14*). Do not grieve the Holy Spirit of God, by whom you sealed for the day of redemption (*Ephesians 4:30*). In Him [Jesus] we have redemption through His blood, the forgiveness of sins, according to the riches of His grace (*Ephesians 1:7*). Fear not, for I have redeemed you; I have called you by your name; You are Mine (*Isaiah 43:1*).

SALVATION FROM THE SAVIOR

To those who have obtained like precious faith with us by the righteousness of our God and Savior Jesus Christ: Grace and peace be multiplied to you in the knowledge of God and of Jesus our Lord (*1 Peter 1:1–2*). Jesus answered them and said, "My doctrine is not Mine, but His who sent Me. If anyone wills to do His will, he shall know concerning the doctrine, whether it is from God or whether I speak on my own authority" (*John 7:16–17*). Whoever believes that Jesus is the Christ is born of God, and whoever loves Him who begot also loves Him who was begotten of Him (*1 John 5:1*). Most assuredly, I say to you, he who hears my words and believes in Him who sent me has everlasting life, and he shall not come into judgment, but has passed from death into life (*John 5:24*). If you confess with your mouth the Lord Jesus and believe in your heart that God raised Him from the dead, you will be saved. For with the heart one believes unto righteousness, and with the mouth confession is made unto salvation (*Romans 10:8–10*). "For God so loved the world that he gave His only begotten Son, that whoever believes in Him should not perish but have eternal life (*John 3:16*). "To Him [Jesus Christ] all the prophets witness that, through His name, whoever believes in Him will receive remission [cancellation of a debt] of sins" (*Acts 10:43*). And we have seen and testify that the Father has sent the Son as Savior of the world (*1 John 4:14*). But grow in the grace and knowledge of our Lord and Savior Jesus Christ. To Him be the glory both now and forever. Amen (*2 Peter 3:18*).

BEING MADE NEW

He who covers his sins will not prosper, but whoever confesses and forsakes them will have mercy (*Proverbs 28:13*). Cast away from you all the transgressions which you have committed, and get for yourselves a new heart and a new spirit (*Ezekiel 18:31*). As many as received Him [Jesus], to them He gave the right to become children of God, to those who believe in His name: who were born, not of blood, nor of the will of the flesh, nor of the will of man, but of God (*John 1:12–13*). Now therefore, you are no longer strangers and foreigners, but fellow citizens with the saints and members of the household of God, having been built on the foundation of the apostles and prophets, Jesus Christ Himself being the chief cornerstone, in whom the whole building, being fitted together, grows into a holy temple in the Lord, in whom you also are being built together for a dwelling place of God in the Spirit (*Ephesians 2:19–22*). You also, as living stones, are being built up a spiritual house, a holy priesthood, to offer up spiritual sacrifices acceptable to God through Jesus Christ (*1 Peter 2:5*). Nevertheless we, according to His promise, look for new heavens and a new earth in which righteousness dwells (*2 Peter 3:16*). Then He who sat on the throne said, "Behold, I make all things new" (*Revelation 21:5*). Therefore, if anyone is in Christ, he is a new creation; old things have passed away; behold, all things have become new (*2 Corinthians 5:17*).

SING OF HIS GREAT GOODNESS

They [one generation to another] shall utter the memory of Your [the Lord's] great goodness, and shall sing of Your righteousness (*Psalm 145:7*). Make a joyful shout to God, all the earth! Sing out the honor of his name; make His praise glorious (*Psalm 66:2*). "I will sing to the LORD, for He has triumphed gloriously!" (*Exodus 15:1*). You have delivered me from the violent man. Therefore I will give thanks to You, O LORD, among the gentiles, and sing praises to Your name (*2 Samuel 22:49–50*). Speaking to one another in psalms and hymns and spiritual songs, singing and making melody in your heart to the Lord, giving thanks always for all things to God the Father in the name of our Lord Jesus Christ (*Ephesians 5:19–20*). Let the word of Christ dwell in you richly in all wisdom, teaching and admonishing one another in psalms and hymns and spiritual songs, singing with grace in your hearts to the Lord (*Colossians 3:16*). Oh, give thanks to the LORD! Call upon His name; make known His deeds among the peoples! Sing to Him, sing psalms to Him; talk of His wondrous works! Glory in His holy name; let the hearts of those rejoice who seek the LORD! (*1 Chronicles 16:8–10*).

FROM TROUBLE TO TRUST

LORD, in trouble they visited you, they poured out a prayer when your chastening was upon them (*Isaiah 26:16*). O LORD, do not rebuke me in Your anger, nor chasten me in Your hot displeasure. Have mercy on me, O LORD, for I am weak; O LORD, heal me, for my bones are troubled. My soul is also greatly troubled (*Psalm 6:1–3*). You, who have shown me great and severe troubles, shall revive me again, and bring me up again from the depths of the earth. You shall increase my greatness and comfort me on every side (*Psalm 71:20–21*). God is our refuge and strength, a very present help in trouble. Therefore we will not fear (*Psalm 46:1–2*). This poor man cried out, and the LORD heard him, and saved him out of all his troubles (*Psalm 34:6*). Though I walk in the midst of trouble, You will revive me; You will stretch out Your hand against the wrath of my enemies, Your right hand will save me (*Psalm 138:7*). The wicked watches the righteous, and seeks to slay him. The LORD will not leave him in his hand, nor condemn him when he is judged (*Psalm 37:32–33*). I will be glad and rejoice in Your mercy, for You have considered my trouble; You have known my soul in adversities, and have not shut me up into the hand of my enemy; You have set my feet in a wide place (*Psalm 31:7–8*).

EXCEEDING INEXPRESSIBLE JOY

This is the day the LORD has made; we will rejoice and be glad in it *(Psalm 118:24)*. Though the fig tree may not blossom, nor fruit be on the vines; though the labor of the olive may fail, and the fields yield no food; though the flock may be cut off from the fold, and there be no herd in the stalls—yet I will rejoice in the LORD, I will joy in the God of my salvation. The LORD is my strength; He will make my feet like deer's feet' and He will make me walk on my high hills *(Habakkuk 3:17–19)*. Rejoice in the LORD, O you righteous! For praise from the upright is beautiful *(Psalm 33:1)*. The LORD reigns; let the earth rejoice *(Psalm 97:1)*. But let all those rejoice who put their trust in You; let them ever shout for joy, because You defend them; let those also who love Your name be joyful in You *(Psalm 5:11)*. Make a joyful shout to the LORD all you lands, serve the LORD with gladness *(Psalm 100:1–2)*. Let Israel rejoice in their maker; Let the children of Zion be joyful in their King *(Psalm 149:2)*. Sing aloud to God our strength; make a joyful shout to the God of Jacob *(Psalm 81:1)*. Oh, that men would give thanks to the LORD for His goodness, and for His wonderful works to the children of men! Let them sacrifice the sacrifices of thanksgiving, and declare His works with rejoicing *(Psalm 107:21–22)*. The LORD has done great things for us, and we are glad *(Psalm 126:3)*. Do not sorrow for the joy of the LORD is your strength *(Nehemiah 8:10)*. Until now you have asked nothing in My name. Ask, and you will receive, that your joy may be full *(John 16:24)*. Whom [Jesus] having not seen you love. Though now you do not see Him, yet believing you rejoice with joy inexpressible and full of glory, receiving the end of your faith—the salvation of your souls *(1 Peter 1:8–10)*. "Rejoice because your names are written in heaven" *(Luke 10:20)*. Let the righteous be glad; let them rejoice before God; yes, let them rejoice exceedingly *(Psalm 68:3)*. Rejoice always *(1 Thessalonians 5:16)*. Rejoice in the Lord always. Again I say, rejoice *(Philippians 4:4)*! Now to Him who is able to keep you from stumbling, and present you faultless before the presence of His glory with exceeding joy, to God our Savior, Who alone is wise, be glory and majesty, dominion and power, both now and forever. Amen *(Jude 1:24–25)*.

MIND YOURSELF

The natural man does not receive the things of the Spirit of God, for they are foolishness to him; nor can he know them, because they are spiritually discerned. But he who is spiritual judges all things, yet he himself is rightly judged by no one. For "who has known the mind of the LORD that he may instruct Him?" But we have the mind of Christ (*1 Corinthians 2:14–16*). But even if our gospel [good news] is veiled, it is veiled to those who are perishing, whose minds the god of this age has blinded, who do not believe, lest the light of the gospel of the glory of Christ, who is the image of God, should shine on them (*2 Corinthians 4:4–5*). For to be carnally minded is death, but to be spiritually minded is life and peace (*Romans 8:6*). And you, who once was alienated and enemies in your mind by wicked works, yet now He [Jesus] has reconciled in the body of His flesh through death, to present you holy, and blameless, and above reproach in His sight—if indeed you continue in the faith, grounded and steadfast, and are not moved away from the hope of the gospel [good news] which you heard (*Colossians 1:21–23*). And do not be conformed to this world, but be transformed by the renewing of my mind, that you may prove what is that good and acceptable will of God (*Romans 12:2*). Let this mind be in you which was also in Christ Jesus,...made Himself of no reputation, taking the form of a bondservant... He humbled Himself and became obedient to the point of death, even the death of the cross (*Philippians 2:5–8*). Commit your works to the LORD, and your thoughts will be established (*Proverbs 16:3*). Be anxious for nothing, but in everything by prayer and supplication, with thanksgiving, let your requests be known to God; and the peace of God, which surpasses all understanding, will guard your hearts and minds through Christ Jesus. Finally, brethren, whatever things are true, whatever things are noble, whatever things are just, whatever things are pure, whatever things are lovely, whatever things are of good report, if there is any virtue and if there is anything praiseworthy—meditate on these things. The things which you learned and received and heard and saw in me, these do, and the peace of God will be with you (*Philippians 4:6–9*). Therefore gird up the loins [center strength] of your mind, be sober, and rest your hope fully upon the grace that is to be brought to you at the revelation of Jesus Christ; as obedient children, not conforming yourselves to the former lusts, as in your ignorant; but as He who called you is holy, you also be holy in all your conduct (*1 Peter 1:13–15*).

FOREVER AND FORWARD FOCUSED

But Jesus said to him, "No one, having put his hand to the plow, and looking back, is fit for the kingdom of God" (*Luke 9:62*). Not that I have already attained, or am already perfected; but I press on, that I may lay hold of that for which Christ Jesus has also laid hold of me. Brethren, I do not count myself to have apprehended; but one thing I do, forgetting those things which are behind and reach forward those things which are ahead. I press toward the goal for the prize of the upward call of God in Christ Jesus (*Philippians 3:12–14*). Remember Lot's wife [looked back and she became a pillar of salt] (*Luke 17:32*), do not turn aside from following the LORD, but serve the LORD with all your heart (*1 Samuel 12:20*). Therefore you shall be careful to do as the LORD your God has commanded you; you shall not turn aside to the right hand or the left. You shall walk in all the ways which the LORD your God has commanded you, that you may live and that it may be well with you (*Deuteronomy 5:32–33*). Let your eyes look straight ahead, and your eyelids look right before you. Ponder the path of your feet, and let your ways be established. Do not turn to the left or the right; remove your foot from evil (*Proverbs 4:25–27*). Let us lay aside every weight and the sin which so easily ensnares us, and let us run with endurance the race that is set before us, looking unto Jesus, the author and finisher of our faith, who for the joy set before Him endured the cross, despising the shame, and has sat down at the right hand of the throne of God (*Hebrews 12:1–2*). Love does no harm to a neighbor; therefore love is the fulfillment of the law. And do this, knowing the time, that now it is high time to wake out of sleep; for now our salvation is nearer than when we first believed. The night is far spent, the day is at hand. Therefore let us cast off the works of darkness, and let us put on the armor of light. Let us walk properly, as in the day, not in revelry and drunkenness, not in lewdness or lust, not in strife and envy. But put on the Lord Jesus Christ, and make no provision for the flesh, to fulfill its lusts (*Romans 13:10–14*).

BROUGHT NEAR, CLEANSED, FORGIVEN, AND GOD'S OWN

But now in Christ Jesus you who once were far off have been brought near by the blood of Christ (*Ephesians 2:13*). The new covenant, in My [Jesus's] blood which is shed for you (*Luke 22:20*). Him [Jesus] who loved us and washed us from our sins in His own blood (*Revelation 1:5*). Much more then, having now been justified by His blood, we shall be saved from wrath through Him (*Romans 5:9*). How much more shall the blood of Christ, who through the eternal Spirit offered Himself without spot to God, cleanse your conscience from dead works to serve the living God? (*Hebrews 9:14*). Therefore, brethren, having boldness to enter the Holiest by the blood of Jesus, by a new and living way which He consecrated for us, through the veil, that is, His flesh, and having a High Priest over the house of God, let us draw near with a true heart in full assurance of faith (*Hebrews 10:19–21*). If we walk in the light as He is in the light, we have fellowship with one another, and the blood of Christ Jesus His Son [God's] cleanses us from all sin (*1 John 1:7*). And you being dead in your trespasses and the uncircumcision of your flesh, He has made alive together with him, having forgiven you all trespasses, having wiped out the handwriting of requirements that was against us, which was contrary to us. And He has taken it out of the way, having nailed it to the cross (*Colossians 2:13–14*). The Son of Man must be lifted up [crucified on the cross] that whoever believes in Him should not perish but have eternal life (*John 3:14–15*). They crucified Him [Jesus] (*Luke 23:33*). Christ died for our sins (*1 Corinthians 15:3*). "To Him [Jesus] all the prophets witness that, through His name, whoever believes in Him will receive remission of sins" (*Acts 10:43*).

Who [Jesus] was delivered up because of our offenses, and was raised because of our justification (*Romans 4:25*). When he had by Himself purged our sins, sat down at the right hand of the majesty on high (*Hebrews 1:3*). He [God by Jesus] made us accepted in the Beloved. In Him [Jesus] we have redemption through His blood, the forgiveness of sins, according to the riches of His grace (*Ephesians 1:6–7*). That having been justified by His [Jesus's] grace we should become heirs according to the hope of eternal life (*Titus 3:7*). He has delivered us from the power of darkness and conveyed us into the kingdom of the Son of His love, in whom we have redemption through His blood, the forgiveness of sins (*Colossians 1:13–14*). For it pleased the Father that in Him [Jesus] all the fullness should dwell, and by Him to reconcile all things to Himself, by Him, whether things on earth or things in heaven, having made peace through the blood of His cross (*Colossians 1:19–20*). Now may the God of peace who brought up our Lord Jesus from the dead, that great Shepherd of the sheep, through the blood of the everlasting covenant, make you complete in every good work to do His will, working in you what is well pleasing in His sight, through Jesus Christ, to whom be glory forever and ever. Amen (*Hebrews 13:20–21*).

BETROTHED BELOVED BRIDE

For your maker is your husband, the LORD of Hosts is His name; and your Redeemer is the Holy One of Israel; He is called the God of the whole earth (*Isaiah 54:5*). Therefore, my brethren, you also have become dead to the law through the body of Christ, that you may be married to another—to Him who was raised from the dead, that you should bear fruit to God (*Romans 7:4*). "I will betroth you to Me forever. Yes, I will betroth you to Me in righteousness and justice, in loving-kindness and mercy; I will betroth you to Me in faithfulness, and you shall know the LORD (*Hosea 2:19–20*). My beloved is mine, as I am his (*Song of Solomon 2:16*). I am my beloved's, and his desire is toward me (*Song of Solomon 7:10*). Make haste, my beloved (*Song of Solomon 8:14*). As the Father has loved me, I also have loved you; abide in my love. If you keep my commandments, you will abide in my love, just as I have kept my Father's commandments and abide in His love (*John 15:9*). He who loves father or mother more than Me is not worthy of Me. And he who loves son or daughter more than Me is not worthy of Me (*Matthew 10:37*). Listen, O daughter, consider and incline your ear; forget your own people also, and your father's house; so the king will greatly desire your beauty (*Psalm 45:10–11*). The Spirit and the bride say, "Come!" and let him who hears, say "Come!" And let him who thirsts come. Whoever desires, let him take the water of life freely (*Revelation 22:17*). "I will call them My people, who were not My people, and her beloved, who was not beloved" (*Romans 9:25*). "Eye has not seen, nor ear heard, nor have entered into the heart of man the things which God has prepared for those who love Him" (*1 Corinthians 2:9*). Therefore, beloved, looking forward to these things, be diligent to be found by Him in peace, without spot and blameless; and consider that the long suffering of the Lord is salvation—as also our beloved brother Paul, according to the wisdom given to him, has written to you (*2 Peter 3:14–15*). For I [Paul] am jealous for you with a godly jealousy. For I have betrothed you to one husband, that I may present you as a chaste virgin to Christ (*2 Corinthians 11:2*). As the bridegroom rejoices over the bride, so shall your God rejoice over you (*Isaiah 62:5*). "Come, I will show you the bride, the Lamb's [Jesus Christ's] wife." And he carried me away in the Spirit to a great and high mountain, and showed me the great city, the holy Jerusalem, descending out of heaven from God, having the glory of God. Her light was like a most precious stone, like a jasper stone, clear as crystal (*Revelation 21:9–11*).

TOGETHER FOR GOOD

He who loves his brother abides in the light, and there is no cause for stumbling in him (*1 John 2:10*). Behold, how good and how pleasant it is for brethren to dwell together in unity! (*Psalm 133:1*). Endeavoring to keep the unity of the Spirit in the bond of peace (*Ephesians 4:3*). As iron sharpens iron, so a man sharpens the countenance of his friend (*Proverbs 27:17*). Speaking the truth in love, may grow up in all things into him who is the head—Christ—from whom the whole body, joined and knit together by what every joint supplies, according to the effective working by which every part does its share, causes growth of the body for the edifying of itself in love (*Ephesians 4:15–16*). Now you are the body of Christ and members individually (*1 Corinthians 12:27*). That you stand fast in one spirit, with one mind striving together for the faith of the gospel (*Philippians 1:27*). Let us consider one another in order to stir up love and good works, not forsaking the assembling of ourselves together, as is the manner of some, but exhorting [strongly encouraging] one another, and so much the more as you see the day approaching (*Hebrews 10:24–25*). "Where two or three are gathered in My name, I am there in the midst of them" (*Matthew 18:20*). You are no longer strangers and foreigners, but fellow citizens with the saints and members of the household of God, having been built on the foundation of the apostles and prophets, Jesus Christ Himself being the chief cornerstone, in whom the whole building, being fit together, grows into a holy temple in the Lord, in whom you also are being built together for a dwelling place of God in the Spirit (*Ephesians 2:19–22*). "He who is not with Me is against Me, and he who does not gather with Me scatters (*Luke 11:23*)."

SAFE, RESTORED, AND RESTED

Turn us back to You, O LORD, and we will be restored; renew our days as of old (*Lamentations 5:21*). Restore us, O God; cause Your face to shine, and we shall be saved! (*Psalm 80:3*). "For the gentiles shall seek Him, and His resting place shall be glorious" (*Isaiah 11:10*). Then He arose and rebuked the wind, and said to the sea, "Peace be still!" and the wind ceased and there was a great calm (*Mark 4:39*). The LORD is my shepherd; I shall not want. He makes me to lie down in green pastures; He leads me beside the still waters. He restores my soul; He leads me in the paths of righteousness for His name sake (*Psalm 23:1–3*). And He [Jesus] said to them, "Come aside by yourselves to a deserted place and rest for a while (*Mark 6:31*). Rest in the LORD, and wait patiently for Him (*Psalm 37:7*). "Come to Me all you who labor and are heavy laden, and I will give you rest. Take My yoke upon you and learn from Me, for I am gentle and lowly in heart, and you will find rest for your souls. For My yoke is easy and My burden light" (*Matthew 11:28–30*). Return to your rest, O my soul, for the LORD has dealt bountifully with you (*Psalm 116:7*). I will both lie down in peace, and sleep; for you alone, O LORD, make me dwell in safety (*Psalm 4:8*). My people will dwell in a peaceful habitation, in secure dwellings, and in quiet resting places (*Isaiah 32:18*). For thus says the LORD GOD, the Holy One of Israel: "In returning and rest you shall be saved; in quietness and confidence shall be your strength" (*Isaiah 30:15*).

TELL THEM WHAT GREAT THINGS THE LORD HAS DONE

"I [God the Father] will also give You [Jesus God the Son] as a light to the gentiles, that You should be My salvation to the ends of the earth" *(Isaiah 49:6)*. He [Jesus] said to them. "I must preach the kingdom of God to the other cities also, because for this purpose I have been sent" *(Luke 4:43)*. And this is the testimony: that God has given us eternal life, and that life is in His Son. He who has the Son has life; he who does not have the Son of God does not have life *(1 John 5:11–12)*. And we have seen and testify that the Father has sent the Son as Savior of the world *(1 John 4:14)*. "Nor is there salvation in any other, for there is no other name [The name of Jesus] under heaven given among men by which we must be saved" *(Acts 4:12)*. "For whoever is ashamed of Me and My words, of him the Son of Man will be ashamed when He comes in His own glory, and in His Father's, and of the holy angels" *(Luke 9:26)*. Let the redeemed of the LORD say so *(Psalm 107:2)*. Then Jesus said to them, "Follow Me, and I will make you become fishers of men" *(Mark 1:17)*. And always be ready to give a defense to everyone who asks you a reason for the hope that is in you, with meekness and fear *(1 Peter 3:15)*. Walk in wisdom toward those who are outside, redeeming the time. Let your speech always be with grace, seasoned with salt, that you may know how you ought to answer each one *(Colossians 4:5–6)*. Now then, we are ambassadors for Christ, as though God were pleading through us: we implore you on Christ's behalf, be reconciled to God. For He [God the Father] made Him [Jesus, God the Son] who knew no sin to be sin for us, that we might become the righteousness of God in Him *(2 Corinthians 5:20–21)*.

"Go home to your friends, and tell them what great things the Lord has done for you, and how He has had compassion on you" (*Mark 5:19*). "Thus it is written, and thus it was necessary for the Christ to suffer [be crucified for our sins] and to rise from the dead the third day, and that repentance and remission of sins should be preached in His name to all the nations, beginning at Jerusalem. And you are witnesses of these things" (*Luke 24:46–48*). And Jesus came and spoke to them, saying. "All authority has been given to Me in heaven and on earth. Go therefore and make disciples of all the nations, baptizing them in the name of the Father and of the Son and of the Holy Spirit, teaching them to observe all things that I have commanded you; and lo, I am with you always, even to the end of the age" Amen (*Matthew 24:18–20*).

ABOUT THE AUTHOR

Ed Lannin loves the Word, both living and written, being especially thankful for lifting him from depression when he was a young adult. Ed is a Vietnam veteran and his hobbies include antiques and disc golf. He has worked various jobs from baking to HVAC sales. He lives in northern Michigan with his wonderful wife of forty-one years and is proud of and enjoys spending time with his three grown sons, their wives, and eight grandchildren.

CPSIA information can be obtained
at www.ICGtesting.com
Printed in the USA
FFHW020815130619
52971794-58588FF